Happily Retired

Price $20.^{00}

Happily RETIRED

What works...what doesn't

Julie Chahal
Linda Lucas

Happily Retired

www.happily-retired.com

U.S. Edition

ISBN: 978-0-557-05791-7

Printed in Canada and the United States of America

Cover photo by Igor Dmitriev

Cover design by Julie Chahal

Contents

Happily Retired

Introduction

The great gift of retirement is freedom. The great challenge for most of us is deciding what to do with that freedom.

Many resources are available to help handle financial planning, relationship problems, health issues, making travel arrangements, organizing projects, and time management. This book addresses the challenges that remain even after you have mastered that list.

Happily Retired provides field-tested pointers for successfully shifting from work to retirement. We offer:

- Strategies to help you make the most of these years while avoiding common pitfalls.

- Ways to apply and balance the three critical components for happiness.

- Practical ideas for how to bring enjoyment, new people, new experiences, and fulfillment into your life – perhaps in ways you had not previously considered, or just forgotten.

- Clarification of some of the less obvious and rarely discussed aspects of retirement, including why people are often ambivalent about this wonderful, exciting stage of life.

Our suggestions are based on observation and personal experience, with some research to fill in the gaps where we needed to know more or wanted to confirm our assumptions. We share what works, and what doesn't.

Retirement is cause for celebration. Consider all that you have seen, learned and done during roughly half a century of life. You undoubtedly worked hard, shouldered responsibilities and successfully handled many life challenges. You earned your retirement. Now you can reap your reward.

Retirement may feel like a leap into the great unknown. Immersed in a busy working life, you may have dreamed of an escape from the less pleasant aspects of work, relief from tension, and endless lazy afternoons. After the big trip and a few projects, the glow wears off.

Many retirees are surprised to find themselves facing anxiety, boredom and disappointment. This often happens as they become stuck in the early and inevitably less satisfying phases of retirement. Some are tempted to pretend that all is well while privately asking, "Is that all there is?" and "What will I do with the next twenty years?"

Role models may be hard to find. These days, new retirees can look forward to decades of vitality. While a sedentary, restful retirement lifestyle may have been appropriate for our parents' generation, baby boomers are redefining what it means to be retired.

Retirement requires that you once again – and maybe for the first time in a very long time – take charge of your own life. It is a fresh opportunity for passion and self-exploration, but you may need some new strategies to create a satisfying life tailored to you.

> The best day of your life is the one on which you decide your life is your own. No apologies or excuses. No one to lean on, rely on or blame. The gift is yours – it is an amazing journey – and you alone are responsible for the quality of it. This is the day your life really begins.
>
> Bob Moawad, author of *Whatever It Takes*

What's Ahead?

Here is an overview of what you will find in the book:

- What to expect in the early stages of retirement and some common misconceptions.

- General strategies. If retirement is going to work for you, you need to first figure out what matters most to you, give yourself permission to experiment, accommodate natural cycles, and fine tune your attitudes.

- The Happiness Formula developed by researchers in the field of Positive Psychology. We demystify the three key ingredients of pleasure, engagement and meaning.

- Ways to bring more pleasure into your life. For many of us simple pleasures are a lost art.

- Ways to cultivate engagement. Engagement may be pleasurable, but it also involves other factors, such as feeling challenged and connected. We provide many examples of rewarding sources of engagement that fall under the broad and overlapping categories of relationships, paid and unpaid work, learning, and hobbies.

- Ways for finding meaning. Definitive answers would be suspect, but we hope you will find some of our observations thought provoking and inspiring.

Throughout the book we have included exercises. Not all of them will appeal to everyone, but some are bound to work for you. A particularly useful tool referenced throughout the book is journaling, introduced in chapter three.

Most chapters include a selection of books and other resources that we have found valuable.

Our Stories

Our own experiences are the primary inspiration for this book. Each chapter contains our personal reflections about how the findings and suggestions have played out in our own lives.

The Eager Retiree: Julie's Story

I had a successful career by most standards, but became dissatisfied despite my title, salary, staff and corner office. Too often I would be proud of an accomplishment only to see it evaporate in the next round of reorganizations or legislative changes. The other aspects of my life (teenaged children, self-professed neglected husband, aging parents, community involvement) needed a lot more of my attention. I wanted more control over my time, my process and my products. I caught myself calculating how many years until I would qualify for a full pension. Wishing my life away did not seem healthy.

 I chose to leave my government career while still in my forties, intending a kind of hiatus from regimented work, a chance to revitalize. I wanted to try something new before it was too late. I planned to give myself a year to get on top of my non-career responsibilities and another year to "play", trying new things and exploring my options. This stage actually took quite a bit longer than planned.

I hesitated to take on this project since most books about retirement seem to have been written by financial planners or psychologists. I am no expert in either of those areas. I do however have some experience as a change agent in large and small organizations and a lifetime of observing others' and my own inner workings.

The Reluctant Retiree: Linda's Story

I confess that I am someone who has not taken well to the idea of being "retired". I did not retire in the usual way – working somewhere for 40 years and then getting a gold watch. Instead, at age 49, I took a "buy-out" from the community college where I had worked for fifteen years – enough years to acquire a small pension, but nowhere near a point where I was ready to stop working.

While many people experience reaching a pinnacle in their career at this age, I did not. I was not happy in my work and really wanted a change. Because my job involved working with technology, and I had some background in training – I felt I had good skills to take to the marketplace at that time. The "buy out" allowed me to collect a year's salary as I explored new territory. It was time to try something new.

Once I made this decision, the reality of not having a regular pay check hit home. In the first weeks after "retiring", I went into a mild depression. One of the biggest challenges was finding a new identity. How did that work? So much of our lives are taken up with our work situation and pursuing a career. It struck me that fifty is not an ideal time to begin reinventing yourself. I felt like I was in free-fall – I had nothing to hang on to. Eventually I found a satisfying second career as a consultant.

Now – at age 60 – I am retiring again. This time I am happy to move on – but just like the first time, I am struggling with the identity question and with needing to figure out what to do with the rest of my life. My earlier experience gave me a good understanding of some of the issues that people face in retirement. My research, sharing with friends, and a certain amount of personal exploration have provided additional answers.

chapter one

Retirement for Beginners

You may not have thought a lot about what retirement actually involves. During your career and with many years still to go, the vision of a happy escape teasing somewhere on the horizon is appealing, reassuring and enticing.

Yet, far from being just a time of rest and recreation, retirement has many different dimensions. What we experience in retirement is influenced by financial resources, lifestyle choices, health factors, relationships, our interests and attitudes. Just like work, some aspects of retirement are good and some are "opportunities for personal growth."

The Great Escape

For most people, retirement often starts out with a bang, but at some point, things begin to fizzle. If you have been retired for several years you have probably already hopped, skipped, or jumped your way through these phases more than once. If you are new to retirement, here's what is ahead along with a few clues about when you might want to move on to something else.

Phase 1: Taking Time to Pause

Immediately after retiring, most people set aside time for an extended vacation. Whether you choose to travel or laze at home, this stage is hard to distinguish from any other holiday taken during normal working life. This period is about decompressing. It is a time of transition, a time to shift gears and clear space for a new phase of life. Usually in this phase you are not too worried about what comes next.
Vacations are a well-deserved part of retirement.

But sooner or later, holiday-mode just doesn't feel right – much like eating only dessert without a main course. If you have always thought of retirement as an endless vacation and don't realize that it is just one of the early phases of retirement, you may feel let down and disappointed. You know you are ready to move on to something else when you start feeling bored and vaguely embarrassed about how you spend your time.

Take as many vacations as you want, but don't turn them into a chore and don't expect them to be your main focus. Vacations are the condiments, not the whole meal.

Phase 2: Cleaning House, etc., etc., etc.

Unfinished business can also consume a lot of your time. You have probably accumulated a list of tasks you will get to – if you ever find the time. When vacationing wears thin, most retirees tackle this to-do list with a vengeance.

Your list may include items such as cleaning the basement, landscaping the yard, painting the deck, creating a personal Web site, organizing files, sorting through photos, or arranging spices in alphabetical order.

Funny thing, though, as you work your way down the list, the tasks become less important and somehow less satisfying. Did you really work all those years with a plan to spend your retirement organizing photos? Of course, tasks that really need to be done will keep cropping up. The question is how much time and energy should they consume. Some of the tasks will provide a genuine source of satisfaction, but beware. Reluctance to move on from this phase gives rise to the stereotype of an aging fuss-budget.

Phase 3: Getting Down to Busyness

"Keep busy" is one piece of advice you may hear frequently. ("Relax" is the other common advice, but most of us quickly get bored with perpetual relaxation, so "keeping busy" is the alternative.)

Work provided the comfort, as well as the annoyance, of routine. Days were organized into clearly labeled blocks of time. At some point, you will want to regain some of the structure and rhythms of your pre-retired life.

In this phase of retirement you sign up for classes, join the gym and block out time to exercise, set-up a regular day for playing bridge or golfing, join new groups, make standing appointments, and schedule time for specific activities. Busyness increases as others seek to benefit from your availability (babysitting the grandchildren, landscaping your nephew's yard, becoming a traveling companion to a lonely friend). You may welcome these additional tasks as proof that you are still in demand.

Once again your calendar is crammed with entries. You wake up in the morning with plans for the day. Your friends begin to complain that you are hard to reach, and that they never see you now that you are retired.

Schedules are helpful, but too much busyness can be exhausting and stressful, and push out valuable opportunities for enriching your life. One danger is over-commitment – keeping yourself so busy that there is little time left for reflection or spontaneity. You should also be alert to the possibility that you are filling your days to overflowing to avoid deeper feelings and awareness.

Phase 4: Big Books and Big Projects

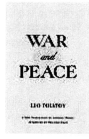

Retirement is also a chance to live your dream. It might be something ambitious – like sailing around the world in a seventeen-foot pocket cruiser – or something less intense like reading *War and Peace* from cover to cover (really reading it, not just relying on Cole's notes and the 1956 movie version that once helped get you through a Russian literature class) .

You may have developed a lengthy list of alluring places to tour and sights to see: the Mayan Ruins of Palenque, Morocco's Atlas Mountains, the Spoleto Festival in Italy, the Great Wall of China, or Turkey's Hagia Sophia. Maybe you want to learn to play the guitar, buy a cottage, write a book, redecorate the house, or research your family tree. Perhaps your personal dream is to open a bed-and-breakfast, start a catering business, run a marathon, or lose forty pounds.

This big project can become a highlight of your life. It can bring focus, new skills, friendships, recognition, vitality, something to discuss at cocktail parties, and an identity. On the other hand, it can be overwhelming. Sometimes retirement projects work out, and sometimes they don't. Some are a lot of work. Most don't last forever. Then what's next?

Not everyone has this kind of dream project. If you do get involved in such a project, be sure that it is a true personal ambition. A common mistake is to succumb to what others think you *should* want to do. Relatives and friends may prod you into doing something because they want to live vicariously through you – or maybe they are just trying to be helpful. Regardless, their encouragement may distract you from recognizing what you really want to do.

As a worker you grew accustomed to seeing projects through to completion, even when the process was unpleasant, even when you questioned their value, and even when real success seemed unlikely. You do not have to do that anymore! Don't let this undertaking become a chore.

Hitting the Doldrums

The belt of calm near the equator was named by early sailors as "the doldrums". It was an area where their sailing vessels might get stuck because of long periods with no wind. The term has come to mean a period in our lives characterized by stagnation, listlessness, a slump.

These four common phases of retirement will appear again and again, but eventually endlessly cycling through these phases without moving onward will lead to lethargy and feeling irrelevant. When how you spend your time seems pointless and frivolous, like a sailboat without wind, you have hit the doldrums.

Boredom is an aspect of this, but in itself boredom is not the problem. Often, people seem to feel shame about being bored, as if it is a failure of sorts. True, these feelings can be uncomfortable, but we need periods of rest and reduced stimuli to recharge. Boredom is an empty space and a chance to change direction. Without it, we might never take positive action to find something new, expand horizons, take chances, or make the effort to learn.

Experiencing the doldrums is perfectly normal. They are an invitation to reconsider who you are and what you want to do. Despite the discomfort, they need to be celebrated as a golden opportunity to redesign or refine the next phase of your life. The major purpose of this book is to offer some ideas on how to do this.

Contemplating Boredom

"Boredom, ...as a form of tedium, often drives creativity, inspiring artistic and scientific innovations and achievements. The issue is how we respond to boredom: We can avoid boredom, in which case we develop habits of distraction. Or we can heed our boredom, and develop habits of attention....

Many of us are bored and don't even realize it because we've masked it. There's a lot of self-deception that goes with boredom, which may be why it's such an underreported and widely misunderstood phenomenon.... If we stick with our boredom and listen to it, we may feel empty, but it can lead to a peaceful equanimity, a freedom from the pull of particular things."

Michael L. Raposa in *Boredom and the Religious Imagination*

Personal Reflections

Julie

I went through extended versions of all the early stages of retirement. The whole family went on a five-week road trip that provided a psychological break from the workplace. I reconnected with friends and family and then tackled my long list of tasks: redecorate, fitness program, renovate the kitchen and bathrooms, sort files, set up a home office, prepare fancier meals, etc. Yes, my spices are now in alphabetical order.

Keeping busy is usually easy for me. I often find myself more scheduled and over-committed than when I had a boss. If I'm not careful, I end up with lots of urgent tasks and no time for what really matters and for taking advantage of spur-of-the-moment opportunities.

I had fun and indulged myself. This included bridge, hiking, and joining groups to meet interesting new people and try new activities. I took on a number of "big projects". Even after being retired for many years and going through all the phases, I regularly fall into the dreaded void of the doldrums.

The hardest period came a few years into retirement. On the one hand, I was quite content with a number of successfully completed projects. I was feeling good that my sons were well underway in their lives, finances in order, no health issues, lots of friends and activities. Doesn't sound like the doldrums?

Well, no one seemed to need my help. I was questioning if my volunteer work actually made a difference. I was bored with activities I had mastered to my satisfaction. I felt like the world had lost interest for me, and vice versa.

Linda

Since I didn't retire in the usual way, I did not have a clear picture of the "beginner phases" retirees typically cycle through – but I can see the truth of this based on the experience of many friends. My full-time work life did not end in the usual sense. Instead, at age fifty I became a consultant. This involved many peaks and valleys with respect to how much work was on my plate at any given point. Summers were typically slow, but extended vacations were precluded by the need to be available for work opportunities.

Although I have now cut back significantly on my consulting work, a challenge for me will be to "allow" retirement to happen. I seem to have a compulsive need to feel productive 80% of the time. Since reality falls far short of that, I regularly experience bouts of the doldrums.

chapter two

Rethinking Retirement

"Thought is the sculptor who can
create the person you want to be".
Henry David Thoreau

Getting Rid of Stereotypes

You may have stopped working full time at a job, but do you think of yourself as retired? Surprisingly few boomers respond with an enthusiastic "Yes!" Responses are more likely to be "sort of", "temporarily", "practicing but not committed", followed by a quick change of topic. "Hemi-demi-semi retired" is one of our favorite responses, a clear indication that the individual needed to assure himself (and others) that he is not quite ready to trade in his laptop computer for a hammock.

Although many hesitate to call themselves retired, others recognize that many preconceptions about retirement are stale and outdated.

People retire younger than they did in previous generations, they are more affluent, and they live longer. The concept of retirement today includes both the young retiree with an energetic lifestyle and older, more physically restricted seniors. With ages ranging from fifty to 85, retirees are a broad and very diverse group.

Too often, retirement is linked to the concept of aging, rather than the idea of freedom and the beginning of another exciting stage of life. Maybe it is time to rethink the definition of "retirement".

> "When a person decides to retire, they are older and they seem to associate retirement with the end of life. We need to change this notion. Retirement should be considered the beginning of another stage of life, not an ending."
>
> Five Ways to Prepare for Retirement
> http://retireplan.about.com

The word "retirement" has both good and bad connotations. While our pre-retirement (admittedly unrealistic) expectation may be that every day can be just like Saturday, negative associations with retirement abound. One problem is that the word retirement itself defines what is essentially a new phase of life in terms of the old life. The dictionary definition uses phrases such as *leaving* a career, *stopping* work, *being away* from a busy life and *withdrawing* from the world. These do not exactly suggest a vigorous or purposeful life. The definitions claim that retirement is really about something left behind. Retirement is defined in terms of inactivity, a former life, a finished career! As a result, we start out on this potentially exciting new venture by assuming the identity of a "has been."

Because words frame how we think about things, typical assumptions about the word retirement itself – and certainly out-of-date ideas – must be discarded if we are to make a fresh start and embark upon a new lifestyle. The trick is to move past the typical negative pre-conceptions and learn to think about retirement differently.

Retirement is not so much about "leaving", it is about "arriving". Work may have "stopped", but a new venture has "started" and retirement is not about "being away", it is about "being." Most importantly, it should be about being happy. While this statement might seem superficial, it is in fact a starting point for determining your new path in life.

Henry Ford said it best: "If you think you can or you think you can't, you're right!" Positive attitudes and expectations produce positive experiences while negative outlooks reduce our expectations and breed disappointment. Retirement offers you a chance to live according to your own priorities and values, rather than someone else's.

Still, you may be unprepared for the gamut of emotions experienced once the delight of not having to race for the morning bus has passed and the doldrums set in.

Plusses and Minuses

Retirement, just like employment, is likely to involve both pluses and minuses. Ups and downs are to be expected, although the doldrums can leave you feeling temporarily pessimistic.

Acknowledging what you have lost and what you may gain can help you gain perspective.

Retirement Downsides

Wasteland

Washed up

No new tricks!

DEAD END

Retirement Upsides

Freedom

Creativity

Fun!

CHOICES

Think of retirement as *withdrawing* from:

- Earning money as a major consideration
- Living by imposed rules
- Externally imposed routines
- Limitations of many sorts

It does not mean the end of productive work, learning, and meaning.

Bumps in the Road

Each of life's big transitions can result in some disorientation. We lose something familiar and encounter a rapid expansion of possibilities. If you are feeling particularly anxious about retirement, recognize that this stage of life is a huge transition.

Laying a foundation for creating happiness in retirement may need to start by recognizing what has been lost. Here are some of the challenges that we face when we leave the full-time workforce.

Loss of Familiarity

Did you ever move into a new house and find yourself rattling around for the first several weeks before the house really seemed like your own? This same loss of familiarity occurs when you retire. In this case, your day-to-day living seems somehow out of sync. Once you leave work, you are bound to miss having a daily routine, a place to go, tasks to perform and a role to play. Establishing a comfortable routine in retirement may take some time.

Loss of Social Context

Being around others helps us feel connected. Colleagues are not necessarily our closest friends, but if you worked somewhere for a number of years you probably enjoyed workplace social gatherings and spending time with a few of the people you got to know. If you are more of a loner and have not formulated any particularly close relationships with colleagues, you will likely still miss the office banter and just being around people who know you. Ready-made social contacts, such as those we experience in the workplace, are not easily replaced.

Loss of Identity

The loss of identity that accompanies leaving the workforce can be a major challenge. This is a big one – and it really does not matter if you were the Grand PooBah or a lowly minion. Spending decades in the workplace is bound to have an impact on your sense of who you are. Remove yourself from the work environment and you are sure to have at least a few moments of anxiety. This is particularly true in an era when society places so much emphasis on having a career. The common introductory question "What do you do?" is a way of gauging a person. Just knowing what a person does for a living can tell us something – and sometimes quite a lot – about that person's interests, aptitudes, and economic and social status. Naming the type of work we do is one way of presenting ourselves to the world.

Our workplace identity has a deeper, personal dimension as well. Our sense of ourselves is caught up in how we spend time daily and in the network of social relations we have with workplace colleagues. In some cases, identity is wrapped up in a successful career. In other situations, a work identity might be built around being experienced and knowledgeable about the company (a mentor for younger workers), being a good listener, being a solid team player, being a hard worker – or being the resident curmudgeon! After many years, you may have grown tired of your work and are genuinely looking forward to retirement but, as long as you are employed, just showing up for work each day still defines a big part of who you are. Experiencing the loss of a comfortable identity can be traumatic. The feelings are a little like those we experience when grieving the loss of someone dear to us.

Discounted

"I have recently retired from a residential post in education, am long divorced and live by the sea with my dog. When friends (couples) and my married daughter come to visit, they 'take over' my situation and house completely. It seems I have no idea or topic of conversation worth listening to, and that everything I do can be improved upon by them. I dish out tea and sympathy with nothing in return. In my job, colleagues supported each other; I miss the whole way of life. I want to enjoy retirement, but being made to feel worthless is not fun."

Jenny as quoted by Dr. Cecilia d'Felice.
"How to be Happy". *The Independent Online Edition*. May 6, 2007

Letting go of the past

Whether positive or negative, you need to come out of the shell of your professional identity and make way for new experiences. That includes relinquishing grievances, memories (good and bad), status symbols, and victories and defeats that were part of your life in the workplace. Pay attention to how often your former work life shows up in conversations.

You also need to let go of relationships that no longer contribute value to your life and roles that are no longer relevant. If retirement has coincided with your children becoming adults and moving out, or with the break-up of a marital relationship (not uncommon), let go to make room for the person you can become.

Part of what keeps us stuck in the past are the scripts that we replay over and over in our heads. Letting go of the past cannot be forced, but be aware of how energy for moving forward is dissipated by re-playing old memories, carrying on a mental conversation with someone who is no longer a vital part of your life, or continuing to focus on past events. Not letting go keeps us from being fully alive in the present.

Moving On

Once you have successfully let go of the past, you enter a kind of no-man's land that can at first seem empty and confusing. Because transitions require psychological adjustment, they take time. North Americans tend not to engage in formal "rites of passage" so important in some societies, but major transitions, including retirement, require a re-birth. We need to acknowledge and respect the process. Allow at least two years to get the hang of retirement. The transition calls for a spirit of adventure and a willingness to be once more cast in the role of a beginner.

Upcoming chapters will explore some strategies for making the most of our time, but first recognize you will need to replace the lost workplace identity with a new and **positive** definition of who you are. Retirement offers an opportunity to shape the future and possibly to discover something new about ourselves.

> "When one door of happiness closes, another opens; But often we look so long at the closed door, that we do not see the one which has been opened for us."
>
> Helen Keller

Compare your own experience of life in the workplace with that of your retirement. Divide a blank sheet of paper into four sections. Write down the things you found positive about work in one section and record the negatives about work in another section. Then think about and record the negatives and positives about retirement in the remaining sections.

If your list of "goods" and "bads" seems unbalanced in favor of work, think about something concrete that you can do to address one or two of the negatives of retirement and add a few positives.

Personal Reflections

Julie

I must admit that I often avoid actually saying that I'm retired. I do run a small consulting business preparing business plans and otherwise working with entrepreneurs, coaching individuals through career changes, and contributing to assorted other projects. I earn some money at this, but one important benefit I derive from the business is having an answer to the question of "What do you do?"

To say that I'm retired is just a negation, telling what I don't do. I no longer have a short answer. I have many long answers, but who will stay to listen? When meeting new people, I have begun to ask different questions such as "What occupies your attention these days?"

Linda

One day I turned in my resignation. The next day I panicked. I experienced various highs and lows over the next few months as the date of my departure loomed. In retrospect I realize that I was having a full-blown identity crisis. Theoretically, I still had over ten years of a career ahead of me . . . but what exactly was I going to do?

Shortly after I left the college, I had what I consider a prophetic dream. Vaguely depressed and still not knowing what my future path would be, I dreamt that I was frantically knocking on the door of the college asking to be let back in. My plea was refused, but as I stood there, the door opened several times, each time to allow someone in to remove the body of someone who had died inside. This was a traumatic dream for me, but reassuring in a way. It made me realize that I had left for a good reason. I needed change and renewal. I think retirement offers this.

⇒ Sheehy, Gail. *New passages: mapping lives across time.*
Toronto: Random House of Canada, 1995.

⇒ Sheehy, Gail. *Understanding men's passages: discovering the new map of men's lives.* New York: Random House, 1998.

⇒ Bridges, William. *Transitions: making sense of life's changes.*
Cambridge, MA: Da Capo Press, 2004

Happily Retired

chapter three

Rediscovering Who You Are

*"Your vision will become clear only when you
can look into your heart. Who looks outside,
dreams; who looks inside, awakens."*

Carl Jung

A big opportunity in retirement is to peel back those layers of social conditioning through introspection. Making a successful transition from work to retirement includes, among other things, the need to delve beneath your workplace identity. So much of who we are is long forgotten territory. As children, we learn to hide our feelings when we are hurt and to stifle our enthusiasm and willingness to take risks for fear of making mistakes. We are conditioned to move cautiously and to fit ourselves into a mold based on the expectations of our parents and teachers and the images of perfection that come to us through the media. As adults we are re-shaped by our relationships, by family and community responsibilities and by our work. So much of what we believe about ourselves is determined by our circumstances and by the opinions of those around us.

There are many fascinating and rewarding ways for self-exploration. The suggestions that follow are just a few possibilities.

Asking Good Questions

A simple question can sometimes yield surprising results. We tend to take a lot of day-to-day ups and downs in stride without probing for deeper meaning. The right questions can help you find a path in retirement that reflects your identity and supports you emotionally:

- When do I feel most happy?
- What memories make me feel good?
- What do I most regret?
- How do I like to spend my time?

What other probing questions emerge as you contemplate the positives and negatives in your life? What do your answers tell you about what's important in life? Are you spending time doing what you love?

If you sit down and ponder these questions, some inner voice will whisper answers. Check for authenticity. An authentic response to these questions will not be subject to judgments driven by "shoulds" and can sometimes involve conjuring up painful memories as you peel away the layers of who you are not. The questions are not intended to elicit a justification for how you have lived your life. They are intended to encourage thinking at a deeper level about the real you.

Definitive answers to all or any of these questions are not required before you formulate a strategy for the future. That process may take months or even years before you feel you are satisfied with your answers. Take your time. Just starting to think about your feelings, your likes, dislikes and talents will set you on the road to self-discovery. If you like, you can record your answers in a notebook or journal. Keeping these questions in your mind and writing down your insights and reflections will help you sort through options and set priorities.

Here are some other things you can do to get better acquainted with yourself.

- Schedule time for yourself. Time alone gives you perspective and allows your inner voice to be heard. Finding a time and place for quiet reflection brings clarity and vision.

- Take a workshop designed to build self-awareness. These can provide insights and, if nothing else, provide diversion and an opportunity to meet new people.

- Start writing (or recording) your memoirs. Explore your memories as a way of rediscovering things about yourself that you may have forgotten.

Keeping a Journal

A journal is an excellent tool for self-discovery. Even if you just record random thoughts and ideas, re-reading those thoughts later can reveal interesting patterns and spark new ventures. A journal can be a memory box of what is meaningful to you.

Keeping a journal can help:

- Clarify feelings and develop thoughts. Journaling is a safe way to vent feelings, clear mental cobwebs, and ease out of psychological ruts.

- Find solutions to problems by offering new perspectives. Journaling offers time to really focus on an issue. The actual process of writing engages the brain in a different way than just sitting and thinking.

- Reduce stress. Writing something down on paper allows you to mentally let it go.

- Clarify goals and find direction. Declaring goals, even if only to yourself, can be a big step toward reaching them. The journal provides a place to step outside immediate circumstances or events and focus on deeper meanings.

- Make time for self-discovery.

Journaling Process

A journal, in the sense we are discussing, is not literature, memoirs, or even grammatical sentences. If you are not initially comfortable with the idea of keeping a journal, you can start by writing down interesting thoughts and ideas as they occur to you

Write something every day at a time and in a place where you will not be disturbed. The something can be anything at all; it doesn't even have to be writing. If you prefer, print, doodle, draw flowcharts, scribble angry slashes, or repeat the same word over and over.

The empty page can be daunting. Consider recording feelings, insights, goals, irritations, dreams, stories, memories, lists, likes, dislikes, words of a song, wishes, anecdotes, hopes, regrets, plans, ideas, poems, etc. Your journal is a good place to capture reactions to what you are reading and to do the exercises in this book.

Journaling Tips

- Develop a habit of writing in your journal every day. It helps to place your journal where you will see it every day.
- Daily entries don't have to be long.
- If you miss a day or several, just pick up where you left off.
- Ignore spelling, grammar and appearance.
- Don't censor content.
- Be completely honest with yourself.
- Keep the pages private, at least in their raw form.
- If you are having trouble getting started, start with a question or explore a memory.

Once you are comfortable with using a pen and paper (or other journaling technique) to record your thoughts, you can move to using a journal for deeper reflection. Because retirement, in many ways, means reinventing yourself, questions about who you are and what's important in your life are bound to surface. If you record your thoughts in a journal, you will be able to revisit them, expand on some and recognize when something no longer rings true. You will find other opportunities for journaling suggested in upcoming chapters.

Morning Pages

A specific approach to journaling is to write three pages every day, ideally first thing in the morning. This discipline can become a relatively accessible form of mental clearing or introductory form of meditation. It's a bit like a morning shower for the brain!

The practice of morning pages invites a kind of thought dump – a place to just let your thoughts, feelings and impulses spill onto the page in a stream of consciousness fashion. Anything that comes to mind goes onto the page. When you use a journal in this way, the gems often appear at about the third page, after you have emptied your mind of seemingly inconsequential surface thoughts.

Make it a Habit

Your journal can become like a friend or mentor that encourages and keeps your life in perspective. Over time you will find yourself less stressed as you release trivial issues that often clog mental space. You may also find yourself fascinated by what you discover about yourself.

> "A journal is a friend that is always there and is always a comfort. In bad moments I write, and usually end up feeling better. It reflects back to me things that I can learn about my world and myself."
>
> Jennifer Moon, author and educator

Use a journal to discover your inner-self. Get a notebook or set up another method for journaling. There are no rules. You decide what to write and when to write.

If writing is not easy for you, you can use a tape-recorder to explore ideas and later transfer your main thoughts to a journal for easier review. You can also collect your thoughts with a computer using a word processor, journaling software, or even e-mail messages to yourself!

When you encounter writer's block

Here are some more questions you can pursue. Keep writing – anything – until journaling is a habit!

- What do you really appreciate about being retired?
- What activity or incident brought you real enjoyment in the past week?
- Describe a memory that always makes you smile.
- What has given you real satisfaction? Explain why.
- Explore the lyrics of a song you love and why they are meaningful to you.
- Whom do you admire? Why?
- What do you regret that you would do differently given another chance? How would you handle the situation differently now?
- Is there something from your work life that you are still angry about? Describe the person or incident and then reflect on why it still has a hold on you.
- How and with whom do you like to spend your time?
- What are your skills?
- What are your unique gifts?

What's Your Type?

Personality typing systems can help you explore your own psychology and better understand what makes other people tick. Typing systems, such as Myers-Briggs, True Colors and even astrology or "What Breed of Dog are You?" can help you see patterns that reveal underlying motivations. Are you an extrovert or an introvert, a leader or a follower, a perfectionist or a free spirit? You have probably investigated personality typing many times before, but we encourage you to revisit this approach as a way of getting new insights and further exploring dimensions of yourself. Try one that you may not have tried before, such as the Enneagram, a system which categorizes people into nine different personality types and explores the relationships among them.

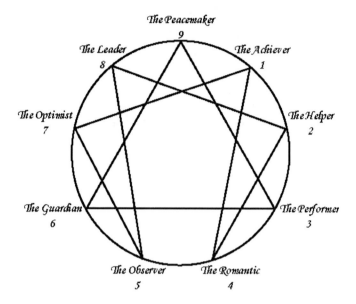

With most systems, you may find traces of yourself in more than one of the types. While personality typing typically identifies distinct archetypes, we often adapt our personalities to external circumstances. Revisiting the personal characteristics described by the typing systems is another exercise in peeling away the layers of social conditioning. Once you are aware of your type, you can work to capitalize on your strengths and better address issues that arise around the negatives. As a bonus, personality typing systems can help you better understand the personalities of others.

Typing systems are systematic ways to explore your psychological make-up. To the extent that you feel confident in the results of a personality test, the results can help you find direction and discover deeper motivations. They are tools that you can use to help bring your identity into focus.

Personal Reflections

Julie

"I already know who I am, what matters to me, and what I enjoy." The first time I said something like this I was twelve years old. Of course, I soon realized that I had just scratched the surface of who I was. Being slow to learn, I repeated this sentiment at several stages of my life. Now I finally realize that I will always have more to discover about myself.

I've kept a journal off and on for a long time. It helps to get upsets off my chest without letting them interfere unduly elsewhere. Even after all these years of experiencing the benefits, I tend to let my discipline slide when all is going well, only to be surprised anew when I go back to writing or doodling a bit each day.

Before retirement I often felt straight-jacketed by responsibilities and expectations – some imposed, but many freely chosen. I don't regret the past; in fact I'm thankful for what it gave me, although at the time I was often exhausted and even resentful.

Retirement has been an unfolding of who I was all along underneath my many roles.

Linda

Several years ago I started encountering the Enneagram as a personality typing system – in employment counseling, at a business seminar, in books and magazines. I wanted to know more, so I took a workshop on the Enneagram. For me they are not a whole lot different from the very scientific Myers-Briggs, but I discovered that many people consider them "New Agey". Reaction to our including a reference to them in the book has been mixed – some people love them (I do) and some people hate them.

What was meaningful for me was that they caused me to think more deeply about the constellation of personalities in my life. I began to have greater empathy for family, friends and co-workers who did not view the world in the same way that I did. Instead of "What, are you crazy?" it was "Oh, I see where you are coming from." Since retirement involves re-evaluating a lot of what makes people tick, I wanted to mention the Enneagram as a useful tool for introspection.

⇒ The practice and benefits of morning pages are described in detail in
Cameron, Julia. *The Artists' Way: a spiritual path to higher creativity.* New York: J.P. Tarcher/Putnam, c2002.

⇒ Computer journaling can be done using a word processor, but you can also purchase a journaling program called "The Journal".
www.davidrm.com

⇒ A source for learning more about Myers-Briggs:
Myers-Briggs Questionnaires and Online Resources:
http://www.teamtechnology.co.uk/tt/t-articl/mb-simpl.htm

⇒ To determine your Enneagram type:
The New Enneagram Test:
www.9types.com/newtest/homepage.actual.html.

⇒ Riso, Don Richard and Russ Hudson. *The Wisdom of the Enneagram: The Complete Guide to Psychological and Spiritual Growth for the Nine Personality Types.* New York : Bantam Books, c1999.

chapter four

Perspectives for Moving On

"I'm not afraid of storms, for I'm learning to sail my ship"

Louisa May Alcott

Once more you are a beginner with things to learn. Even if you have begun the process of self-exploration, adjusting and eventually finding your way to a new beginning will require experimentation. This stage of life calls for determination and a willingness to take risks. The inevitable set-backs call for acceptance, optimism and humor.

Experimentation

Through the process of introspection, you may have developed some ideas about what will make this stage of life satisfying. The next step is to test those ideas by getting out into the world and doing things. You are constructing a new life and exploring new territory. You need to be willing to experiment, and you need to be willing to make mistakes.

This stage of life is a whole new game and you do not yet know what works and what does not. Experimentation is essential, but it can mean occasionally heading down a path that's not right for you. Mistakes happen: moving to the cottage and suddenly feeling isolated and out of touch, or buying an expensive RV and having to admit that this lifestyle is not for you after only one or two trips. Many activities are fun at first, but become boring or unfulfilling after a short time. Even if you did invest in expensive golf clubs, you don't have to feel obliged to play three times a week.

Sometimes the process of taking up something new, and then losing interest and moving on, can seem irresponsible, childish, even embarrassing. Since this is a process of trial and error, welcome even negative results. Don't think of these false starts as mistakes. Think of them as new information that will help you refine your strategy for figuring out what you do want. Discovering what does not work is as valid an experimental result as discovering what does

41

work. In retirement we are testing new choices, and many of these will be discarded.

Be open to experiencing many possibilities. Push your boundaries to refine your preferences. Experimentation helps us grow.

"If you want to grow, put yourself at risk every day. These risks do not have to be big risks; smaller scale risks will work just fine. Things like talking to someone new, reading something you wouldn't normally read, etc. The only criteria is that it should be something you felt a little uncomfortable doing and has the possibility of leading to some new knowledge or experience. If you try something you were afraid to try, you will build your self-confidence, while gaining new information you can use to work towards your goals."

Edward W. Smith in Sixty Seconds To Success

Cycles and Re-cycles

Every ending offers a new beginning, an unfolding in a spiral of experiences building upon whatever has gone before. You cycle and re-cycle through days, weeks and months in a constant whirl of experiences each of which propels you on to the next to form the unique creation that is your life.

Pre-retirement life had many rather straight trajectories. Getting an education, parenting, and career all represent long and largely linear blocks of time. For example, you may have had a series of different but related jobs that gave you a sense of steadily moving forward on a long straight path. Even if you switched career paths, you probably still had a sense of years unfolding as you moved forward in your life.

By comparison, retirement seems punctuated by shorter cycles and an accompanying series of ups and downs. As you experiment, you are bound to feel a bit deflated when things don't work out. Boredom, or even depression, often marks the winding down of one cycle before the next one begins. These are the doldrums described in chapter one. The time between cycles can be uncomfortable, but much more bearable when recognized as a natural lull preceding new opportunities.

While the ups and downs themselves are inevitable, we are better prepared to move forward with confidence when we understand and accept that we are evolving. Hitting a low point signals that it is time again for experimentation.

Pruning

Adjusting to retirement can seem less like an awkward adolescence and more like a gentle unfolding if we recognize the benefits of pruning. Pruning is about cutting back and re-shaping in order to foster new and healthier growth. Gardeners appreciate the need to lop off twigs, branches, roots – anything that seems superfluous or non-productive.

Retirement begins when you sever your job from your life. Other aspects of your life may need a good pruning – getting rid of habits, beliefs, possessions, and even relationships that no longer contribute but continue to deplete energy.

Consider some of the ways that unnecessary clutter might push away opportunities:

- You like to be helpful to family members who ask you to run a multitude of errands for them. Before you know it, your uncommitted time disappears and you have a full calendar with no room for any of the activities you want to do.

- You are loyal to a long-time friend although she has, over the years, become more and more critical of you, telling you what to do, and expecting you to spend a lot of time with her. You meet others that interest you but no longer have the self-confidence or energy to get to know them.

- You have high standards and want to excel at everything you do. Unfortunately, anything new has a learning curve during which you may look less than competent so you prefer not to try.

- You were forced into retirement by an unreasonable boss. You spend sleepless nights fuming and imagining revenge and days complaining about the injustice. Others start avoiding you and you're not having any fun.

Your reactions to situations such as these are choices. Chores, people, standards, stale ideas and negative emotions can be removed to make way for new choices that serve you better. Pruning gives us a chance to re-evaluate and to discard things that are no longer relevant and that may actually interfere with the direction in which we need to grow.

While most of us recognize the different stages in life, we do not always acknowledge the degree to which we have become different people as we age and evolve. Interests change, motivation changes, and our sense of what is important changes. Regularly pruning the deadwood in our lives promotes new growth.

De-cluttering provides an energy boost that must be experienced to be truly believed. Start with a small experiment. Choose a drawer or a shelf or a corner that you have not accessed for a long time (perhaps a month or more). Examine each item and ask yourself if you would buy it today if you saw it in a store. Put back only the yeses and get rid of the rest.

Ask yourself how you feel about the process.

Ask yourself what new possibilities have opened for the use of that space.

This process is most visible with material things, but is every bit as effective with habits, activities, social commitments, address books, grievances, etc.

Acceptance

Another challenge that sometimes must be faced in conjunction with retirement is the need to adapt to a disability, illness or other setback. At a minimum, aging may bring diminishing physical stamina and diminishing influence in the world. Sometimes disability forces us into retirement before we are psychologically ready. A disability is a serious challenge, and much time and energy will necessarily be absorbed in adjusting and coping. Other life-shaking events may be related to financial issues or the departure of a loved one.

All of these bring unhappiness and stress into our lives. A primary goal for anyone facing a life trauma (our own or that of a partner) is to somehow find a way for moving forward.

The Serenity Prayer

"God, give us grace to accept with serenity
the things that cannot be changed,
courage to change the things that should be changed,
and the wisdom to distinguish the one from the other."

Reinhold Niebuhr

The Serenity Prayer is well known and valued by many. Living accordingly remains a challenge. For most of us acceptance is hard, possibly because we equate acceptance with feelings of helplessness. That's a mistake. It is not that we are helpless, it is that a particular set of circumstances is beyond our ability to control in the way that we would like. We may not be able to change a situation, but we can control our responses and our outlook. With its message of acceptance, the Serenity Prayer is a critical step toward healing because it allows us to let go of guilt, feelings of failure and personal responsibility for situations that we cannot change. Even where the current problem is somehow connected to something we may have done in the past, if the situation cannot now be altered, acceptance and forgiveness are essential ingredients for moving forward toward peace and serenity.

Deep disappointments are very real and we cannot always make them go away. Fear, denial, anger and depression are understandable reactions, but are debilitating in the long run. Disability, illness, life's losses do not define who we are or what our life is about. Acceptance, along with a belief in the future, is the key to healing.

The end goal – and the stage at which we begin to heal – is acceptance. Getting to the acceptance stage probably cannot be rushed, but knowing that there is a way through when confronted with a physical impairment or the loss of a loved one can be reassuring. We have no choice but to move on.

Need Inspiration?

"The Diving Bell and the Butterfly" is a film that captures the challenge of moving forward after a profound set-back This is the true and heart-wrenching story of a highly successful and creative man who, as a result of a stroke, finds himself completely paralyzed. Jean-Dominique Bauby is imprisoned in his own body and can only communicate to the outside world by blinking one eye. He realizes that he can still experience life through memory and imagination and he uses these faculties to dictate (though the simplest of eye movements) his memoirs. His memoirs communicate the richness of the inner life that he was still capable of experiencing.

If your spirits need boosting, you can try keeping a "gratitude journal." The rules are simple. In a notebook or journal write down five things for which you are grateful each day. If you are trying this, don't miss a day.

Gratitude journals are especially helpful on days when you are feeling angry, frustrated, or discouraged. This simple process can make an amazing difference to your outlook on life. In fact, researchers have confirmed that taking the time to consciously count your blessings can significantly increase overall satisfaction with life.

Humor

Norman Cousins in his classic work ***Laughter is the Best Medicine*** made a very strong case for the relationship between laughter and health. He attributed his own recovery from a difficult collagen disease to his systematic pursuit of humor. In an attempt to regain his health, he spent day after day watching tapes of humorous movies. Humor made a big difference in his life.

Reports on the emotional and physical benefits of humor are becoming common. Finding something funny is a natural human response, but hardly a one-size-fits-all phenomenon. You will need to gauge what role humor can play, but do make sure that laughter appears often in your life. A good laugh can relieve stress as you adjust to retirement and provide emotional sustenance through those experiments that don't quite work out.

When was the last time you went to a comedy film? When was the last time you read something by Stephen Leacock or Mark Twain? How often does something seemingly serious at the time, become genuinely funny later? The wisdom that comes with aging (although sometimes age comes alone, as the old joke goes) does help us take ourselves less seriously. We may as well laugh and, with practice and attention, we can learn to do it.

Optimism

Learning to be more optimistic can help overcome feelings of helplessness and defeat. But can optimism be learned? Many psychologists say yes. At some level, being an optimist or being a pessimist is based on a choice we make about how to view life's events. An optimist views a negative situation as a temporary setback and does not see it as evidence of personal failure. Optimists strive to see the bright side of things even when situations go awry. Optimists choose not to dwell on negative outcomes. You can move toward a more positive outlook on life when you become aware of habitual negative thought patterns, such as anger, guilt or self-pity. The secret to becoming an optimist is to re-train your brain.

Positive Self-talk

Many therapists recognize that our thoughts, rather than external events, cause our feelings and behavior. The key to better outcomes is to change your thinking. Follow these steps:

- Learn to recognize negative thought patterns. Use the word "stop" to interrupt the thought mid-stream whenever you catch yourself thinking something that is negative and self-defeating. (Saying "stop" out loud makes this technique even more effective.)

- Identify a set of positive mental responses that can be used to "re-frame" in any given situation. (A negative response based on habit or low self-esteem is frequently an overreaction or a distortion.)

- Replace the negative thought with more positive self-talk any time you catch yourself lapsing into a negative emotional spiral. (Examples: "This is challenging, but I know I can deal with it. Even though my feelings are hurt, I am sure it was not intentional.")

Changing the way you are thinking and speaking can change the way you feel.

The notion of positive thinking may provoke cynicism about how much actual control you have over what seem to be natural emotional responses to reality. However, once you are willing to believe in the possibility of deliberately shifting your thinking, you will be tempted to start exploring opportunities and trying new tactics like visualizing a better situation, relaxation techniques and positive self-talk. Blondes may have more fun, but optimists definitely do.

Embracing change

The biggest roadblock to positive change is often the fear of change itself. Change happens all the time, with or without our active involvement. Inviting change entails proactively shaping your own future by taking practical steps to design a more pleasurable, engaging and purposeful life.

Inviting change means considering the possibilities, establishing a direction and stepping into the future. Picture yourself moving forward with confidence and welcoming change into your life.

Personal Reflections

Julie

I don't handle boredom well and gladly pay the price of a bit of stress. I make a point of pushing at my personal boundaries because I fear that otherwise my options will shrink in little ways. A small example of shrinkage, that I am willing to accept, is that I go to some lengths to avoid traveling across town during rush hour. A small example of pushing by trying something new is agreeing to give a speech to a large audience, although the thought makes me nervous.

I love change, at least if I have a measure of control over what is changing and how it happens. The part of the Serenity Prayer that I find the hardest is accepting what cannot be changed.

Linda

I am often willing to try new stuff – even when at first glance it seems a bit goofy. A few years ago I decided I would investigate positive thinking. At the time it was something new – at least if you ignored Norman Vincent Peale who wrote ***The Power of Positive Thinking*** half a century ago. At any rate, it was new to me. I think it is one of those things that is rediscovered each generation.

On a whim I purchased Jack Canfield's set of tapes, ***Self-Esteem and Peak Performance***. I found the affirmations (positive statements) included on one of the tapes especially powerful. I admit that initially I felt a bit silly looking in the mirror and reciting things like "I like Myself" and "My mind is at peace." It was even worse if my husband happened to walk into the room during my ritual.

Doesn't matter – the experience turned me into a true believer. There is nothing magic about "positive self-talk". It is a way of countering all of the negative messages we typically send to ourselves day in and day out. I found that the effect of deliberately reciting more positive messages significantly improved my sense of well-being.

⇒ For a questionnaire that identifies 100 things that you might need to do to improve your life, see the following web site:

> Are you ready to clean up your life?:
> http://www.betterme.org/cleansweep.html

⇒ For a review of the clinical evidence on the benefits of optimism and cognitive techniques designed to foster healthy optimism see:

> Seligman, Martin E. P. *Learned optimism.* New York: A.A. Knopf, 1991.

> MacDonald, Lucy. *Learn to be an optimist : a practical guide to achieving happiness.* San Francisco: Chronicle Books, 2004.

⇒ For a more detailed explanation of positive self-talk:

> CBT: Cognitive Therapy in London:
> http://www.timlebon.com/cbt.htm

⇒ A web site that discusses the benefits of laughter and provides links:

> Humor, Laughter, and Health:
> http://www.helpguide.org/life/humor_laughter_health.htm

chapter five

Strategies for Happiness

*"Happiness . . . impels us through all its mazes
and meanderings, but leads none of us
by the same route."*
Charles Caleb Colton

Retirement is a unique opportunity to re-discover yourself and create
a thoroughly satisfying life experience. Now you have a chance to
build your life around your strengths, interests and passions and
leave behind many constraints. The background strategies discussed
in the last three chapters lay the groundwork for moving forward.

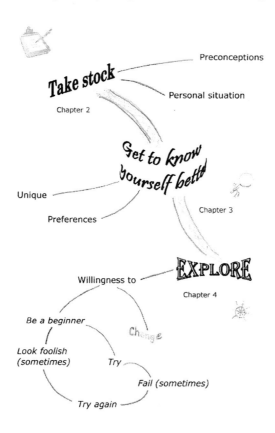

The goal is happiness. Now what's needed is a practical roadmap. What is the best route to a happy life? Fortunately, psychologists have turned their attention to studying the factors that contribute to happiness. They have come up with "The Happiness Formula."

The Happiness Formula

The relatively new field of positive psychology, pioneered by Dr. Martin Seligman, gives us this equation:

$$Happiness = Pleasure + Engagement + Meaning$$

Pleasure

Pleasure is about playing and feeling good in the moment. It's about indulging the senses and having fun. Easy? Some of us have been working so hard that we have forgotten simple pleasures or even rejected them as childish. Pleasant, enjoyable activities can sustain or restore a feeling of well-being. We need pleasures for our mental and physical health and are not likely to be happy without them.

Engagement

Engagement is more intense and longer term. It is about the process of getting involved, developing potential, and striving towards excellence. Engagement requires focus and effort. The emphasis is on the process as much as on results.

Not all engagement is pleasurable. You can be very involved in cleaning your basement after a flood, battling an illness or finding a nursing home for aging parents. All of these involve focus and effort.

When we choose to apply ourselves to an activity that is also pleasurable, we achieve a sense of satisfaction: learning to play the violin; turning a casual interest in photography into a serious hobby;

working hard to improve your tennis game, writing skills, or level of fitness; or choosing a learning vacation rather than a luxury cruise.

With engagement we add another dimension to happiness.

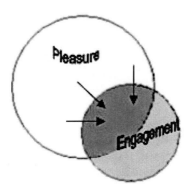

Start with a pleasurable activity, learn more about it, practice the skills to improve performance, and lose yourself in the process. You may enjoy jogging when the weather is good and you have the time (pleasure). You become engaged if you decide to undertake a serious training program that generates a sense of achievement.

Meaning

Meaning is the most challenging aspect of happiness. It is a central motivating force in life with many contributing factors. Philosophers and theologians have struggled with the concept for thousands of years. It is not surprising that we as individuals often struggle to understand meaning and its role in our lives.

Undoubtedly you have many threads of meaning woven into your life: values, family, career contributions, connection to a church or community, helping others. A sense of meaning may be felt in loving and caring and honoring spiritual beliefs, personal expression, excelling, and feeling we are making a unique personal contribution. Meaning requires connectedness and feeling that you matter to a greater whole. This experience provides deep satisfaction.

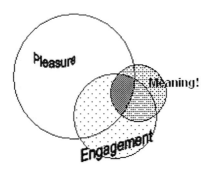

Meaning may combine with pleasure in watching grandchildren grow, experiencing great music, or creating something that of enduring value. Most often, meaning and engagement overlap when we actively participate in areas where the results matter to us. Meaning may combine with engagement, without pleasure, when doing difficult work for a worthy cause. All three may be present when you are actively involved in nurturing your grandchildren.

Putting it together

Seligman's happiness formula is compelling as a way to think about the issues and options of retirement. Retirement offers a new opportunity to explore each of the components: pleasure, engagement, and meaning. Working lives may have been a compromise between wants and needs. Retirement gives us a chance to address aspects of the happiness formula that previously may have been neglected. Ultimately happiness will depend on finding an optimal balance among these three elements.

Although pleasure and engagement and meaning are not likely to be present in equal measure in our lives, to achieve long-term happiness we need to experience all three to some degree. The size of the circles pictured above reflects, not the relative importance of each of these elements, but the degree to which they are likely to be available in our lives. Pleasure should be an abundant and enduring aspect of your life. You need to be focused and selective in deepening your involvement to experience engagement and meaning. Achieving meaning through activities that are relevant and connected to a greater good brings long-term satisfaction and fulfillment.

Pleasure, engagement and meaning are far from clear-cut discrete terms. A specific activity can often fit into any one of the categories or several. Moreover, all of these elements are highly subjective. Only your own interpretation matters. You will determine the values that get plugged into the formula, and how each of the elements best fits into your life. When pleasure, engagement and meaning are all present in your life, the result is happiness. You will feel happiest in those rare moments when these three factors come together in particular activities.

In the following chapters we invite you to explore each of these components of the happiness formula. We offer ideas, big and small, that will help you create your own roadmap to happiness in retirement.

Considering the elements of body, mind and spirit is a common way to seek balance in life. Try combining this concept with the happiness formula using the following matrix.

Prepare a simple table like the one below.

	Pleasure	Engagement	Meaning
Body			
Mind			
Spirit			

Enter current activities and interests that fit into each box. Circle those that you would like to expand. Don't worry if you can't think of something for each of the boxes. Subsequent chapters may spark ideas for filling in some of the blanks.

Personal Reflections

Julie

Finally psychologists are studying what works instead of what keeps us from being happy. As a former student of mathematics, I love seeing formulas. They remove extraneous details. They are clear and elegant and they work.

Linda

I was not previously familiar with the "Happiness Formula," but I was delighted to discover that there is such a thing. This practical, down-to-earth strategy has a ring of truth for me. I can't wait to get started on the pleasure part!

⇒ Seligman, Martin. *Authentic Happines: Using the New Positive Psychology to Realize Your Potential for Lasting Fulfillment.* New York: Free Press, c2002.

chapter six

Finding Pleasure

He who does not get fun and enjoyment
out of every day. . .
needs to reorganize his life.
George M. Adams

Pleasure is that essential component of happiness rooted in the moment and in the senses. Through pleasurable activities, we are energized and bring positive feelings to those around us. Pleasure enhances our ability to experience the world and entices us to pursue new ventures.

If you've been lucky and wise, pleasure has been a continuing part of your life, although pressures of time, money and family responsibilities probably limited opportunities for pleasure during your working life. You may even have forgotten how to enjoy simple pleasures.

Retirement offers fresh opportunities for feeling good, and for enjoying ease, play, entertainment, fun, and laughter. Actively seeking opportunities for pleasure is an important strategy for a happy retirement.

Google It

Stick the word pleasure into a search engine and then DUCK! In today's adult world, pleasure has been reduced to a very narrow band of activity, practiced most vigorously by twenty-somethings. Pleasure is all about SEX. Nothing against sex as a source of pleasure, but if you are not experiencing pleasure in a wide range of contexts, chances are you are overlooking a genuine source of joy in retirement. Somewhere between "childhood play" and "adult XXX" pleasure, lots of folks have lost the capacity to just have fun.

Pleasure can provide benefits on many levels. It may appear to operate on the surface and be fleeting in duration, but the effects go deep and build a foundation for longer-term happiness.

Among other benefits, experiencing pleasure provides a boost to the immune system. How often have you come down with a cold or flu shortly after having a negative experience or setback? Pleasure has the opposite effect.

> "A recent study of 12,982 Swedish residents published in the *British Medical Journal* found that people who regularly attended concerts, theater, art and other cultural events were *twice as likely to be alive nine years later* than those who rarely attended such events. In fact, the study showed that rare attendance at cultural events was *more dangerous than being a heavy smoker.*"
>
> Thomas R Blakeslee
> http://www.attitudefactor.com/pleasure.htm

Pleasure Stoppers

If you are feeling stressed or cranky and life seems lackluster, you are probably suffering from a fun-deficiency. Many retirees remain stingy with the amount of time they allow for pleasure, partly out of habit. For a good portion of our adult lives, our responsibilities forced us to ration the time available for just plain fun. Leisure may have been experienced primarily as a release from negatives; for example, a day off when you could sleep in instead of waking to an alarm and battling rush hour traffic.

Guilt is another factor that can impede our pursuit of pleasure. We are driven by "shoulds" and "should nots". Our lives are governed by serious notions: accomplish something; work hard to get ahead; time is precious. The pursuit of pleasure seems frivolous and undisciplined, even childish. These old fashioned pronouncements remain a part of our thinking, and are not easily shed in retirement. We need to challenge the tendency to associate pleasure with a certain amount of guilt.

Overcoming Reservations

"Unfortunately, many of us tend to feel that too much pleasure is in some way harmful. Perhaps it pulls us away from reality. We feel that the man or woman too involved in pleasure is unable to cope with life. Part of learning how to derive more pleasure out of life consists in overcoming that kind of reservation. The other part lies in doing away with our conviction that if pleasure comes easily, it must be bad... But in reality, undeserved pleasure can do us a world of good."

From *The Pleasure Book* by Julian Fast

Our capacity for pleasure is also diminished when former pleasures become chores or habits. As a retiree, others expect you to enjoy yourself. The pursuit of enjoyment is your just reward after working so hard for so many years. Anything short of wallowing in non-stop pleasure can feel like failure. This is the state of mind that drives people to golf seven days a week and others to engage in relentless travel. Pleasure becomes work if it feels like something you must do. We shouldn't have to work at experiencing pleasure. Pay attention if you catch yourself pretending that you are enjoying yourself more than you really are.

Happiness depends on finding the right balance between pleasure and other pursuits. Pleasure involves variety, newness and a mix of sensual experiences. In the last week, how would you rate your exposure to the following experiences?

Fun-o-meter

Pleasurable Experiences	Want More	Just Right	Examples
Laughter			
Smiles			
Enjoyable time alone			
Social time with pleasant people			
Physical activity			
Something new or different			
Listening to music			
Attending an event or entertainment			
Mental stimulation			
Treat for the senses			
Creativity			
Close to nature			

Ideally, you will want to have some of each type of pleasurable experience regularly in your life. Evaluate the categories where you indicated you experienced too little in the past week. Focus on these areas of pleasure for next week. This may require you to deviate from your regular routine, but that in itself can be enjoyable. Now is the time to balance out years of under-indulgence.

Rediscovering Pleasure

Many different kinds of activities can be a source of pleasure. According to the annual Harris Poll, current favorites are reading, watching television and spending time with family and children. Going to the movies, fishing, computer-related activities, exercise, gardening, walking and renting movies are also popular.

Almost anything that amuses or relaxes us can be a joy – cooking, bicycling, playing bridge, painting, or taking the dog for a walk. There's the pleasure of building sand castles, finding great stuff at a garage sale, indulging yourself for just one night at a fancy hotel, getting a massage, loafing, or having a celebration for no particular reason.

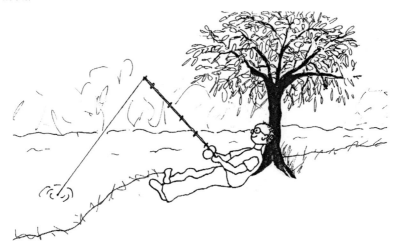

Indeed, pleasure can also be about just doing nothing. While the prospect of doing "nothing" may leave you anxious about boredom setting in, our brains are far too clever for that. When we take time to pause – quietly sitting on a patio or front porch or spending an evening soaking in a tub – creativity, imagination and reflection kick in. By doing nothing you can re-kindle your sense of what it is like to "be in the moment." Doing nothing puts us in touch with ourselves.

More than anything, pleasure is about being in the moment.

> "Oh, I've had my moments, and if I had to do it over again, I'd have more of them. In fact, I'd try to have nothing else. Just moments, one after another, instead of living so many years ahead each day."
>
> Nadine Stair, eighty-five years old, Louisville, Kentucky (as quoted in *Full Catastrophe Living* by Jon Kabat-Zinn, Ph.D.

Being able to fully experience what is immediately happening around us and having a heightened awareness of the sights and sounds in our environment are important aspects of pleasure.

Typically our minds run on overdrive – seeking satisfaction, making plans or worrying. Force yourself to spend twenty minutes today or tomorrow on simply watching the grass grow or sitting quietly in a comfortable chair. If you find this uncomfortable, keep it up until you discover the joy in just being. The experience of being alone without a book, newspaper, T.V. computer or radio can be revitalizing, once you get past the discomfort.

> I notice that voice that keeps asking "What next?" and "What *should* I be doing?" "Nothing," I answer the voice.
>
> "Shouldn't you check email?" "It will wait."
>
> "Shouldn't you do errands?" "They can keep."
>
> I spend time looking out the window at the branches waving in the wind. I suddenly have ideas for three poems — now those are worth the time! I take a walk. I make tea. . . . Tomorrow is a busy day but I have three days in a row after that with no fixed points. What luxury!
>
> Ann McNeal
> Retirement with Spirit, http://retirespirit.blogspot.com/

Remembering Fun

The memory of our experiences of pleasure as children often reveals what are likely to be sources of pleasure for us as adults. If your pleasure-seeking skills are really rusty, you may need to re-learn how to bring fun and pleasure back into your life. Childhood is a time for fun, and most of us have wonderful memories of experiencing pleasure as children.

Memories of fun (from friends and acquaintances)

- Visiting my grandmother in the fall and being served a steaming cup of cocoa with hot buttered crumpets and homemade jam tarts. What a treat!

- Staying out late on a summer night and catching lightning bugs in a jar. Warm summer nights are magical.

- Spending the day at an amusement park with one of those all-day passes; riding the bumper cars over and over again.

- Having sleepovers, listening to Beatles records, staying up until three or four in the morning, and telling ghost stories.

- Jumping rope – especially "double Dutch" once you got the hang of it.

- Learning to play golf with my granddad, heading out with him in the early morning with the mist on the grass and once in a while spotting a deer.

- Helping Mom with the baking – mostly around holiday time. She would let me help her measure things and I would always get to make a mini-something. It was a good way to learn, but most of all I liked spending time with her. And at the end of the afternoon, there were always some great treats.

- Ice-skating. There was a pretty good pond in our neighborhood and all the kids would skate there once it had fozen over. One year we discovered a really icy hillside nearby and a few of us would "ski" down the hill on our ice skates. That was fun until I landed hard on my rump.

- Hanging out with friends at a shopping mall on a Friday night. I still like shopping malls.

- Reading Archie comic books.

- Playing Monopoly.

- Sipping a milk shake.

Find a place where you can be alone without interruptions. Close your eyes and try to conjure up memories of some pleasurable moments from your childhood. What did you love to do? What for you was the most fun? What feelings did you experience when you were involved in this activity? When was the last time you experienced such a feeling? You may want to record your findings in your journal.

Having More Fun!

Pick one of these activities to do this week. Use your "Fun-o-meter" results to select a pleasure area that needs beefing up.

1. Take yourself on a mini-vacation. Block out a morning or an afternoon this week. Think about some place you would enjoy experiencing on your own – a museum, a local park, a restaurant you have been wanting to try, or the local library – especially if you never go to the library. For more ideas, track down a travel brochure for your town. *[Enjoyable time alone, Something new or different.]*

2. If you are a compulsive reader – and can't bear to sit without a book in your hands, try dipping into a book of poetry. Your reading will necessarily slow down and your thoughts will be drawn towards reflection. *[Enjoyable time alone, Mental stimulation.]*

3. Find a new place to walk. If you enjoy walking and typically do a quick jaunt around your neighborhood, deliberately select a new and unusual setting in which to walk. Find an unfamiliar neighborhood or park, or drive to the next town and explore. The newness of the locale will stimulate your sensory enjoyment. *[Physical activity, Close to nature]*

4. Learn to knit. Yeah – you!! Doesn't matter if your grandmother never taught you to knit or you belong to the other sex. Knitting is in. Did you know that knitting was invented by men? There's even a blog for men who knit: http://www.menwhoknit.com/community/. Knitting offers

66

creativity and relaxation for anyone. Best of all, if you make a mistake, it's easy to undo! *[Something new or different, Laughter, Creativity]*

5. Try a new event. Many newspapers have a "What's On?" section that lists concerts, theatre, art openings, lectures, social events and other pleasurable activities. Artists' tours (where you are able to visit a number of artists' studios), house tours (focus is usually on unique or interesting homes), and historical walking tours are all fun. If you live in a city and check out the local event listing, you are likely to find something new to try every week. If you live in a small town or in the country, watch for craft sales, ball games and other community events, or set your alarm for 2:00 a.m. and check out the night sky. Even if you are not sure you will enjoy something, strive to sample some new activity. Things that are new and novel are often sources of

pleasure. *[Something new or different, Attending an event or entertainment]*

6. Make yourself a treat. What kind of food or drink do you especially enjoy? This is not intended to be an ambitious cooking exercise, just an opportunity to provide yourself with a simple treat – real chai tea, a glass of homemade lemonade, old-fashioned s'mores, cheese fondue, blueberry pancakes or a tuna melt. Make sure your treat is something that you do not have every other week – all the better if you invite someone to join you. *[Treat for the senses]*

7. Play a game. Games are a source of both solitary and social enjoyment. Sudoku is for many a delightful mental challenge. If you have never learned to play bridge, take a class or download a tutorial from the Internet. Bridge is both a great way to keep your brain cells from atrophying and an enjoyable social activity. If cards are not your thing, buy a scrabble game and find a partner or join a game online. Many places have trivia competitions – some are sponsored as charitable events. Join a team or invite friends for your own trivia event. *[Mental stimulation, Social time with pleasant people]*

8. Go Geo-caching. Geo-cachers use a Global Positioning System (GPS) and coordinates posted on the Internet to locate

"treasures" hidden in their neighborhood. For many, the thrill is in the challenge of finding the cache and in discovering a nearby place you may never have visited. It's not difficult, and it is a wonderful activity to do with a friend or grandchild. *[Something new, Physical activity]*

9. Put on a favorite CD, lower the lights and listen. Pick out something by a long-forgotten artist or a great musician or singer that you haven't listened to for a long time. If you enjoy music, investigate getting an MP3 player for yourself. These involve a small learning curve, but once you own one, you can select your favorite artists and songs and have them available for listening while you are on the treadmill, at the dentist's office – almost anywhere. *[Listening to music]*

10. Get-together with someone whose company you enjoy. Pleasure does not have to be about a particular activity. Sometimes it can simply involve being around people whose company you like. For most of us, informal get-togethers with friends or family are an abiding source of pleasure. *[Social time with pleasant people]*

Think about something you really love to do . . . and do it. Use the above list for inspiration. You don't need to commit to just a few strategies. Hopefully, you have the resources of experience, time and funds to run some experiments. Pleasure should be a deep well that you can dip into whenever you feel the need for refreshment.

Personal Reflections

Julie

My life is more and more filled with indulgences in how I spend time and money. Yet I think of myself as not being very good at just fun. I seem to get quickly bored when skimming the surface of activities; that is, if I'm not learning or being otherwise productive. Guilt keeps tugging at the edges.

Linda

While writing this book I came across a copy of "The Pleasure Book," by Julian Fast. Fast's book brought back some great memories for me. I remembered once heading out on a snowy evening with my younger brother, Len. What I remember most was our roughhousing in the snow, chewing on chocolate caramels and cracking jokes. It was so much fun. But really, it was all about nothing. This memory brought home to me how pleasure is tied to "being in the moment" – so rewarding and so hard to do.

⇒ A rich and diverse collection of tales about how people experience pleasure (Out of print, but you can order a copy from Amazon.com or get it at the library):
> Fast, Julius. *The Pleasure Book*. Stein & Day Pub (December 1975)

⇒ Online Game Resources:
> Yahoo Games: http://games.yahoo.com/games/front
> MSN Games: http://zone.msn.com/en/root/default.htm
> Web Sudoku: http://play.websudoku.com/
> Lexulous: http://www.lexulous.com/ (online Scrabble)

⇒ Lists of popular leisure time activities:
> The Harris Poll:
> http://www.harrisinteractive.com/harris_poll/

chapter seven

Engagement

"Retirement is about doing what you want,
so if it involves a bit of work so be it."
Derek Foster, **The Lazy Investor**

Beyond momentary pleasures, engagement provides a more lasting satisfaction with pleasure as a potential by-product. Engagement is the difference between skimming the surface and caring enough to really get involved. At first glance, it may look very similar to a simply pleasurable pastime, but in reality engagement is more complex. Engagement generally incorporates these six elements:

- Effort, feeling challenged
- Drawing on and building on strengths and skills
- Sense of accomplishment and even mastery
- Learning
- Enjoyment of the process as much as the results
- Feeling connected

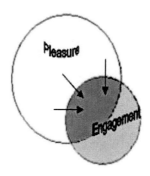

Pleasurable activities can be a starting point for engagement. Pleasurable pursuits often involve interactions with other people and flow easily from our interests and skills – gardening, going to a concert, taking a painting class, joining a bridge group. Momentary pleasures, however, involve only sporadic learning, may not be difficult enough to provide a sense of accomplishment, and seldom offer a sustained sense of connectedness.

Although pleasure frequently is about "enjoying the process," rewards are short-lived. In retirement, a chronic pursuit of pleasure may be an attempt to escape boredom. Our senses are greedy, needing ever more stimuli in order to provide pleasurable feelings. At some point, it is essential to invest ourselves in something beyond pleasure.

A job typically provided engagement in the form of tasks (ideally interesting and well-suited to your skills) that became opportunities for achievement. The challenge in retirement is to continue to find such depth of involvement among activities that you choose. Without investing ourselves in something, we inevitably become chronically bored and also boring.

Finding opportunities to use old and new skills is central to engagement. Through decades of living, learning and working, most of us have a considerable store of skills and talents. Finding new and novel ways to employ our skills and express our talents can be an abiding source of satisfaction in retirement.

When pleasure and engagement merge, the result is "flashes of intense living" in the zone known as flow experiences. "Alienation gives way to involvement, enjoyment replaces boredom, helplessness turns into a feeling of control, and psychic energy works to reinforce the sense of self, instead of being lost in the service of external goals." (Csikszentmihalyi).

Flow = Pleasure + Effort

> **From Pleasure to Engagement**
>
> For years, Bill and his wife took pleasure in playing non-competitive bridge with friends once or twice a month. Two years ago they agreed to pay more attention to their caliber of play. They began to take courses and read books, and seek out others who took the game seriously. Increasingly they participate in and sometimes even organize bridge events, including tournaments. They also teach others to play.
>
> This extra effort has given them satisfaction and a sense of pride in their growing skill. They feel closer to each other in this new kind of partnership and have made many new friends with others similarly engaged.
>
> They have just discovered an added bonus. The director of their bridge club showed them a notice from a cruise ship line looking for leaders of bridge activities in exchange for free cruising. They applied, were accepted, and are packing for two weeks in the Caribbean!

Becoming Engaged

We become engaged when our attention is focused and we are immersed in an activity that stretches our abilities. Ultimately, we are looking for an optimal exchange between effort and accomplishment.

Balance, as always, is the key. Your challenge is to find the right level of challenge.

> *Too little = boredom*
>
> *Too much = anxiety*

Becoming engaged involves identifying areas of personal interest that are ripe for greater involvement. Activities that you most enjoy are a good starting point. The next step is to find a course of action aimed at deepening your interest through learning, skill development, and accomplishment.

One option is to set some goals. "Setting goals" may sound like work, but these are your own. Goals should not be rigid "must-dos", but rather markers on a road-map as you move along the path towards greater engagement. One of the luxuries of retirement is that we can allow the process to matter more than the results, but goals offer a starting point. Goals inspire action.

Goals can be short-term or they can extend over a lifetime. For purposes of becoming engaged, goals may be aimed at a result that will give you a sense of personal satisfaction and accomplishment.

Much of the time, your goals in retirement will focus on building skill or gaining knowledge in an area of expertise or interest. Looking for new ways to use and expand what you already know is often a good starting point.

Area of interest ➜ Goal ➜ Action

Area of interest	Taking Action
Bridge	Taking a class Seeking out opportunities for more frequent play to improve your skill
Music	Building a CD collection for a favorite genre Learning to play an instrument Joining a choir
Healthy lifestyle	Learning more about health foods Starting a part-time business focused on healthy living Seriously pursuing a fitness activity
Travel	Joining a travel group such as "Friendship Force" Volunteering abroad
Computers	Setting up a Web site for yourself or a friend Exploring new computer technologies Teaching a class
Cooking	Exploring new cuisines Publishing your own cookbook for family and friends
Photography	Blocking out more time to take pictures Using online tutorials to learn more about photographic equipment, techniques and opportunities for selling your photographs Seeking out photo exhibits to spark new ideas
History	Joining an historical re-enactment group Planning travel adventures around visits to historic locations
Writing	Exploring story-telling

Engaging Outside of the Box

In the Manhattan Street Project, engagement happens for Mary Sargent when she combines an interest in photography with her interest in exploring new terrain. Mary has set herself a goal of walking every street in Manhattan, taking photos and publishing one photo each night on her blog. In this case, we suspect that a new level of fitness is an added bonus. Visit Mary's blog at: http://newyorkphotoblog.blogspot.com/.

Sometimes engagement evolves naturally. As you become more caught up in an area of interest and gain skill, you are inspired to broaden and deepen your involvement. A casual interest in gardening becomes a passion when you read books, join a gardening group, experiment and make discoveries. An interest in old cars becomes an exciting venture once you join a car club, start your own restoration project or volunteer to help a friend with such a project. If your interests run to the unorthodox, you may need to be more proactive in finding like-minded souls. In this connected world, you are unlikely to be limited by a lack of information.

Finding New Opportunities for Engagement

- Get information from the public library. Many libraries have information about local clubs and carry dozens of special interest magazines.

- Check out bookstores, magazine stands, and of course the Internet. Social networks (like Facebook) and blogs provide new opportunities for interacting with others who may share your interest.

- Look for relevant events through listings in the newspaper, local bulletin boards, and courses or workshops. This is a great way to meet others with a similar interest.

- Subscribe to a magazine that specializes in the area you want to pursue – and be sure to check out the classified ads for unique learning or travel opportunities.

- Post your own notice.

- Mention your interest at social gatherings.

Tip! Start a file for tracking anything that catches your eye. Even if an event, contact person or group is not of immediate interest, this information may prove relevant later on.

Whatever involvement you choose, selectively increasing your psychological investment from casual interest and fleeting pleasure to engagement will bring rewards. The six key elements of engagement (effort, drawing on strengths, etc.) ensure a deeper and more lasting experience. Although lately the word "challenge" has become a code-word for something that must be overcome, in reality we thrive when our undertakings are not too easy. We are inspired by what we do well. Sources for engagement typically reflect our natural strengths, and we feel successful when we reach our goals – large and small. Learning offers a new perspective, new ideas and a sense of renewal. Engagement spurs us on towards accomplishment and feeling that sense of connection.

In upcoming chapters, we will take a closer look at a number of different avenues for engagement: finding new work contexts, volunteering, becoming more involved with friends, learning and pursuing hobbies. Before launching into those chapters, take time to consider what areas of interest or personal skill hold promise for you for finding engagement.

For at least one week, take a few moments at the end of each day to review how you spent time in terms of how engaged you were and how enjoyable you found the various activities.

Investment advisors talk about PE (Price to Earnings) Ratios, but our own version provides a way of relating our investment in the form of engagement to the pleasure we experience. For any activity you undertake, what is the pleasure/engagement ratio? Finding out can provide some useful clues to adjusting how you design your life.

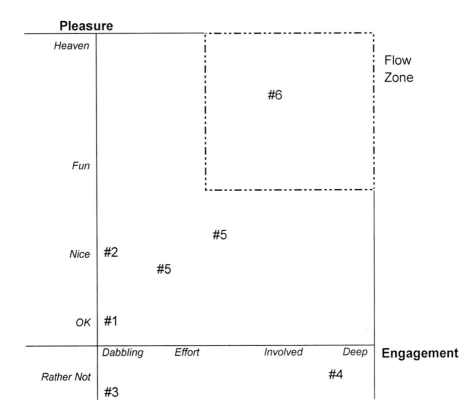

Examples of how to use the grid

1. Low engagement with only modest enjoyment is usually boring.

2. Getting a massage can be very enjoyable and requires very little personal involvement.

3. A dental appointment might be mildly unpleasant, but not require much effort.

4. You can be very involved in caring for a very ill relative, generating satisfaction and learning, but the actual process will often be unpleasant.

5. Reading the newspaper requires little effort, while reading literature can reward the extra concentration with greater enjoyment.

6. Deep engagement combined with pleasure in the process generates a feeling of grace or flow where you lose track of time and personal boundaries disappear.

Interpreting your PE ratio

A well-balanced life will show a spattering of activities covering much of the area that is both pleasurable and engaged. If you are bored, try increasing your level of engagement. If you are feeling over-extended, focus on activities that give you pleasure, pruning others.

Keep checking that your choices are satisfying and that you still have time and energy for just lighthearted fun. Use the grid to identify pleasurable activities that could become a springboard for engagement.

Ideally we engage in what is pleasurable and the engagement produces more pleasure as well as sustained satisfaction. They often do go together, but not necessarily.

Personal Reflections

Julie

I am an engagement junkie. I love to get below the surface to discover how much I already know and can do and build from there. Doing what I do well feels good. Giving appreciated advice feels good. Solving problems feels good. Growth by building on strengths feels good.

I dread the doldrums that inevitably follows completion of any major undertaking, such as this book. I hope I am able to follow my own advice about accepting them as part of the natural cycle and then moving on.

Linda

My problem with engagement is that I suspect I have a short attention span. I am very enthusiastic about new ventures at the start, but then I lose interest and want to move on to something new. My home is riddled with traces of my many abandoned interests – unused skeins of yarn, acrylic paints, stacks of cookbooks, a neglected yoga mat, half-written novels carefully saved on disks that no longer work on my computer. I think that a lot of people are like this. Maybe it's o.k. to be serially engaged. I think it is. All of my former enthusiasms have been enriching in some way.

⇒ Csikszentmihalyi Mihaly. ***Finding Flow: The Psychology of Engagement With Everyday Life***. New York: BasicBooks, c1997.

chapter eight

Friends, Lovers and Others

*"Each friend represents a world in us,
a world possibly not born until they arrive,
and it is only by this meeting
that a new world is born."*
                                        Anaïs Nin

More time for the people in our lives is usually high on the list of reasons to want to retire. We need people at all levels of closeness: acquaintances, companions, close friends and intimates.

While we are all social creatures, the need for different levels of intimacy varies greatly for individuals. Extraverts enjoy a busy social calendar and being surrounded by a buzz of activity. For these people, having others around them is central to their sense of personal validation and well-being. At the other end of the spectrum, introverts may shun casual relationships in favor of having a few close friends. These are self-sufficient individuals who enjoy solitude, take pride in their independence and have no qualms about attending a concert, dining out or even traveling on their own. Most of us fall somewhere between these two extremes. Retirement presents fresh opportunities for evaluating the importance of our relationships, for strengthening existing ties and for making new friends.

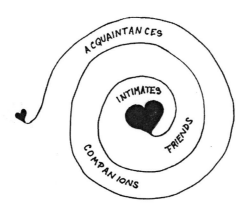

Changing Relationships

Before retirement, many of your friendships may have been closely linked to your work. These relationships may be hard to maintain without the nurturing of daily contact. Colleagues still working may have little discretionary time. You may discover that without work you have few common interests. Some may even be envious of your new freedom. Even friends who retired earlier may be less available than expected. They may have moved, travel extensively, or be immersed in new activities.

Typically, people drift in and out of our lives. Sometimes life circumstances result in formerly good friends becoming just acquaintances. On the plus side, retirement may provide an opportunity to reconnect with likeable people whom you have previously been too busy to get to know.

Casting Your Net

Acquaintances are the people you know casually. You may see them regularly, but may not know them very well. Being surrounded by familiar faces helps us to feel like we are part of a community.

Companions are people you may see often – or perhaps only once or twice a year. You enjoy conversing and doing things together, and may share one or more common interests. Companions are comfortable and add variety to your social life.

Acquaintances and companions form the pool of candidates for finding new friends. Close friendships develop over time and cannot be forced, but if you feel the need for a more substantial social network, you can get the ball rolling by seeking out enjoyable situations that will bring you in contact with more people.

Making the First Move

Sometimes the quickest route to broadening your social network is to take the initiative in getting people together. Organizing an event need not be a big risk nor a lot of work.

Elizabeth wanted to get to know some of her neighbors better, but felt a bit overwhelmed by the logistics and work involved in throwing a party. Instead, she chose a date for dinner at a local restaurant and invited anyone who was interested to come. Ten people expressed interest, and Elizabeth followed up by making reservations. On the day of the event, participants gathered at her home in order to car pool and everyone had an enjoyable evening.

The evening generated enough enthusiasm that a few participants suggested other outings and Elizabeth encouraged them to follow her example. By simply taking the first step, she sparked the opportunity for a number of new friendships.

Strategies for Finding Companions

Here are some additional strategies for fostering friendship in your life.

1. Join a tour. Traveling with a group is a great way to extend your network. On a tour you have an opportunity to travel, eat and interact with people day after day. Over the course of several days, a week, a month or more, you will gradually come to know them. Tours need not be expensive. Short bus tours of a few days are very popular. Don't be put off if the other participants are traveling with a partner and you are not. People on tours are usually interested in getting to know other travelers, so solos usually feel welcome. Reading up on the places you will be visiting provides an easy way to start a conversation. Make sure you trade contact information so you can stay in touch, then follow up with an invitation for coffee or lunch.

2. Join a group. This does not have to be too intrusive in terms of your lifestyle or time. Select a group that reflects something that already interests you: playing cards, investing, cycling, foreign films, bowling, politics. You can find out about formal and informal

groups in your community through the newspaper, community center or at the local library.

3. Take a class. Select a course that is likely to maximize social interaction and time for chatting. A woodworking or Chinese cooking class is likely to offer a more sociable venue than a university lecture course in physics or economics.

4. Start a ritual. Sometimes friends drift apart because no one takes the initiative to get together. Relationships thrive as people spend more time with one another. Set up a regular time to meet a friend and lock it into your schedule. An easy venue is breakfast at a nearby restaurant. Other options are monthly outings exploring a new neighborhood or going to a movie and finishing with a drink. Regular events take less planning. Sharing experiences brings people together.

5. Join a local chapter of Toastmasters. Meet people while improving your public speaking skills. The groups are usually supportive, help you become a better listener and build self-confidence.

6. Volunteer. Consider a children's sports team, local museum, soup kitchens, fundraisers, church activities or similar community projects. Volunteering in a casual setting is a good way to polish your social skills and start making contacts in your community.

7. Check out an amateur theatre group. You do not have to be an actor to get involved in local productions. Behind-the-scenes

volunteers are needed for all kinds of tasks from ticket taking to set construction, to managing the lighting or sound system. Arts festivals, music festivals and sporting events such as marathons provide similar opportunities.

8. Start or find a support group. Support groups are informal groups who meet regularly to exchange ideas and offer mutual support about a common concern. Themes may be coping with an illness, grieving, losing weight, or self-discovery. A support group can offer companionship and a wealth of ideas. A group can consist of as few as three people. Members commit to meeting regularly and the focus is on mutual support. Visit a local community resource centre to help locate a support group in your community or ask for advice about starting one.

9. Resurrect an old friend. Dig out your address book and contact one person you have not spoken to for a long time.

Dipping into the Past

One of the perennial items on Debby's to-do list was to clean up her address book. She finally got started. She came across names that she no longer recognized and were easy to prune. Some, however, were of people she remembered liking a lot, although she had not been in touch with them for years. She contacted one or two by phone, starting the conversation with "I don't know if you remember me." She was amazed that they did remember and were glad to hear from her. The result was that these old contacts were renewed.

Look for social opportunities that promise to bring you in contact with kindred spirits and actively pursue those relationships where you sense a mutual spark. Your best chance of making new friends is to surround yourself with like-minded people. Forget about taking a dance class if you are really a lot more comfortable reading than kicking up your heels, but do think about joining (or starting) a book group. Friendships are built around common interests, and close friendships will take time.

Most important in broadening your social circle is to turn off the television and venture out. Typically, the hardest part about going into an unfamiliar situation is doing it for the first time. Once you push past any initial reservations, most of the time you will be very glad you did. Introduce yourself -- talk to people -- ask questions. Don't expect instant results, and always be on the lookout for new possibilities.

Forging Closer Ties

Close friends are people with whom you are most likely to maintain a relationship over time. You value your time with them and will go out of your way to make sure that connection is not lost. Close friends may share your view of the world. You can count on them to nurture and support you. Retirement usually does not change the relationship with our closest friends, and it can provide opportunities to forge even closer ties. For example, going on a trip with a close friend (or even a casual friend) can develop a deeper connection.

You have probably accumulated a large number of acquaintances, as witnessed by the size of personal address books and stacks of business cards. Before retirement, you may have been too busy to notice how few of the people in your life were something less than close friends. You may even be unconsciously sending out the message that you do not want close ties. Some people are self-protective and, without realizing it, they hold others at a distance. If you sense that this is a problem for you, you will need to make an extra effort to meet people and cultivate friendships. The more often you socialize, the more comfortable you will be with allowing greater intimacy.

Close Friend or Just Friendly?

Friendship is a continuum with no clear demarcations. Here are a few questions to help you discern if someone is more than just an acquaintance:

- Can you call just to talk; that is, without a specific bit of information, question or other agenda item?
- Do you have more than one common goal, interest or activity?
- Can you ask for help or encouragement or analysis of a concern? Is it safe to confide in them?
- Can you name three things you admire about that person?
- Do you know something about and accept each other's weaknesses and imperfections?
- Do you trust them to be kind and to be considerate of you?
- Do you keep in touch regularly?

Deciding that you want to place more emphasis on friendship is often enough to start the process spontaneously. If you are impatient or out of practice, here are some practical steps you can take.

1. Identify an acquaintance that you like or admire.
2. Ask about their interests to see if you have some in common. If you have encountered them in several contexts, you already have a few clues.
3. Suggest doing something together related to that other area of interest.
4. Subtly let them know what about them you admire.
5. Risk exposing some mild concern or weakness about yourself.
6. Wait for some form of reciprocation.

You need to be open to others. Focusing on them, rather than on how you are feeling, will attract people to you and help overcome feelings of shyness. Be a good listener and be generous with your time. Engagement is the magic ingredient to transform acquaintances into friends.

Intimates

Intimates are those with whom we have the deepest connection. Intimates are parents, brothers, sisters and loved ones who know us best and who are an abiding presence in our lives. The closeness we feel to intimates is not dependent on seeing them frequently. They are there. They are a part of us. They are the people with whom we experience an instant connection even after an absence of many months.

Your Significant Other

> *"Retirement is twice as much spouse and half as much money!"*
> *Anonymous*

Like friendships, marital relationships may change in the context of one or both partners retiring. The end of a career, the sudden loss of identity and the disappearance of familiar routines put pressure on both retirees and their spouses. A previously easy-going individual can suddenly become hyper-critical or demanding. In the absence of a broader network of friends and acquaintances, a partner may suddenly be expected to fill all emotional needs.

Some couples find that they have little in common once they no longer share goals in raising a family and paying the mortgage. Irritants in a marriage – possible to ignore when life is busy and children are a priority – may suddenly become a serious strain. Having a lot more time together and fewer pressing responsibilities can be a shock for any relationship. Who is this person you have been living with all these years? When did the two of you shift from being soul mates to being more like ship mates, dealing with routine schedules and mundane tasks? Can you still find intimacy beneath the layers of habit?

Having different visions of the retirement experience can cause surprise and frustration. Your partner may dream of extensive travel while you would prefer to garden at home. Timing of retirement can also have an impact on a relationship. Tensions frequently arise when a husband retires while his wife continues working. This particular combination is likely to shift roles or result in uneven workloads. How household chores should be shared can be a flash point for some couples. Talking about your expectations and negotiating in advance can help avoid disappointment and irritation.

This is a time of reassessment and personal searching. Relationships are almost inevitably a part of that. Be careful to distinguish between general angst related to retirement and genuine problems in a relationship, and be aware that good relationships are not necessarily problem free. Successful relationships are built on communication, compromise and mutual respect. They depend on finding the right balance between togetherness and autonomy. A crisis can sometimes be weathered by finding greater distance and sometimes by fostering more intimacy.

Tips for Good Partner Relations in Retirement

Take time to be alone. Everyone needs personal time for privacy, hobbies and pursuing personal friendships. Time alone replenishes the capacity to give to others.

Make time to be together. Happy couples make time for joint activities, socializing together and intimacy. Retirement provides new opportunities for closeness.

Communicate openly. Make sure that each of you understands the other's vision of retirement. Good communication involves both talking and listening. Beware of patterns that can undermine relationships – bullying, blaming and competitiveness.

Compromise. When conflicts arise, look for the middle ground as a way of resolving them. If you want to travel and your partner does not, what opportunities are there for traveling individually? Come to an agreement about how household chores are shared.

Couple dynamics are beyond the scope of this book, but be prepared for major re-evaluation and renegotiation of many aspects of your relationship. Recognize that new strains on a partnership are quite common among retirees. Retirement also provides an opportunity for the kind of attentive nurturing that can bring about a renaissance in a marriage.

On Your Own

Being single, perhaps after a long time as part of a couple, has its own challenges. Adjusting to losing the social aspects of work, missing spontaneous lunches and after-work get-togethers, can leave you feeling particularly lonely at first. You hear couples complaining about the difficulties of always having a spouse underfoot and you think, "At least you have someone to talk to!" Often, couples like to socialize with other couples, so you are not invited to dinners and outings as much.

The same suggestions apply with respect to getting out there and meeting people with common interests. But now you have another resource in on-line dating sites. They have different categories, depending on whether you're looking for companionship, long-term relationship or "casual encounters". They are a relatively safe way to be introduced to people you wouldn't normally meet, to check out what sorts of people are out there and, most importantly, to get clarity and insight into yourself. In writing your own profile, and reading other people's, you really think about what is important to you, what appeals to you about other people. Unlike when you were young and dating, you have already proven to yourself that you can be independent; you already know what you like and dislike.

Not Settling

Very few of my close friends are married, so we spend time together in various configurations of people. Party guests are counted in people, not couples. Activities with friends who are part of a couple are often done during times when their spouse is doing something else. It does require extra effort, though, because there is no built-in companion. For me, that can be a bonus because I've discovered that I really like the freedom of doing things alone in exactly the fashion that I like. I sometimes think of it like going on a date with myself.

Truth is, I'd like to have a great committed relationship. If it's not great, why bother? I'm grateful that I don't have to go through the discomfort of making a relationship based on who-I-was-in-the-past work now. I figure that the best way to attract the right person to me is to get on with being the person I want to be.

Ruth Redekop
Accountant, Bodyworker, & Meditation Teacher

Engaging with Offspring

Retirement often occurs in tandem with children leaving the nest. Hopefully your grown children still care about you and enjoy your company, but the irony of successful parenting is that they no longer *need* you. They are usually more interested in hearing you acknowledge their accomplishments than in receiving advice.

A big challenge is to step out of old patterns when interacting with children. When they first leave home, they are struggling with the need to prove their ability to take on adult responsibilities. Your advice may not be welcome. You may have thought that cleaning up your daughter's apartment would be a nice surprise, but she is very likely to take it as a criticism and consider it an invasion of her privacy. Parents must learn to respect their children's autonomy.

You need to be innovative in finding new ways to connect. Create opportunities for getting together, start new rituals and build on old family traditions. Parents may need to make an effort to learn more about their children's interests and work. Having good listening skills and being open to sharing your knowledge and skills can encourage closeness and mutual caring.

Most importantly, don't lose perspective. Young adults need to sever the ties of dependence on their parents, and sometimes this involves a period of acrimonious interactions (commonly experienced during the teen years, but not entirely gone in the years after that). If you model living happily, children will hopefully be eager to learn from you, or at least to be willing to be in your company.

Creating Space

Not all relationships with adult children result in "happily ever after" scenarios. Sometimes your best effort may not be enough. Occasionally personality clashes (like two Alpha males) are tolerable when children are younger, but intractable once a child becomes an adult.

An added complexity occurs when adult children become involved with a partner. You may be very accepting of the new relationship, but the new partner may not be quite so welcoming, creating the risk that your child may get caught in the middle of an emotional tug-of-war.

All of us are bewildered and stressed when our children get into difficulties, such as the loss of a job or a marriage break-up. Create an emotional buffer zone between yourself and whatever may be going on in your child's life. You can't solve their problems for them, and they may resent your trying to do so. Keep the door open and let them know that they are always welcome but, at this point in your life, make sure that your focus is on retaining your own health, happiness and well-being.

Grandchildren

For many, grandchildren are one of life's big bonuses with the potential to bring pleasure, engagement and meaning into our lives. They provide models for sensuality, play, creativity, and enthusiasm for learning. They give us a larger context and often help us discover aspects of life that are fresh and new.

For grandchildren, grandparents are also very significant. Grandparents can provide reassurance in difficult situations and they can help children formulate a positive view of life.

Retirement provides more time to cultivate these relationships but, like other relationships, connecting with grandchildren can be complex. Family disputes, distance and an obvious generation gap can create obstacles.

Even where relationships are not easy, cultivating a permanent bond with a grandchild is usually worth the effort. A valuable strategy is to try to deal with each grandchild as an individual, creating contexts in which the child is the sole focus of your attention. For example, start an annual tradition of taking each child, alone, on a shopping trip or to a favorite restaurant – something that they would anticipate and treasure year after year.

Forging Ties with Grandchildren

- Be respectful to them. Often adults are not, and they really appreciate it. Listen carefully and respond.
- Remember things that are important to them and ask about them — a project they are working on, a friendship, an activity, a test at school.
- Keep in touch with them directly. Call them; send them postcards, greeting cards, and email.
- If they don't live nearby, send them mail every week. Children like to get mail. They hold onto it, re-read it and show others. They might keep it forever. One of my grandchildren still has postcards I sent to her weekly when she was 3 - 8.
- Write them heartfelt notes now and then (at least yearly). Tell them all the positive things you can think of about them. Tell them how much you value the relationship and remind them of things you have done together.
- Keep their secrets. Children really need a grownup they can tell everything to who won't get angry or tell their parents. Of course, if it is something dangerous, you must tell, but let them know you have to tell.
- Teach them something — baking, sewing, repairing, building, cooking. They will have a great memory and you will have given them a great gift.
- Don't criticize them at all. Offer your ideas and help direct them, but criticism pushes them away.

Rosemary Mazurek, M.S.S.A., A.C.S.W.
Psychotherapist
(and Grandmother Extraordinaire)

Draw concentric circles representing different levels of intimacy on a large piece of paper with a symbol for yourself in the middle. Enter the names of or symbols for the people in your life within the appropriate circle. On the outer edges might be names of groups that form your pool of acquaintances. How do you feel about the picture that emerges? Which of your acquaintances or companions are possible candidates for closer friendship?

Personal Reflections

Julie

Close relationships are the center of my life. Everything else pales in comparison.

As a result of my introverted tendencies, I have a small but dense core of intimates. I have always given the nurturing of these relationships a high priority, no matter what else was going on in my life. As someone who enjoys people and a wide variety of activities, I have a very large number of companions and acquaintances with whom I am friendly.

The range between intimates and companions has changed the most since retirement. While employed and raising a family, I just didn't have available the considerable time and energy required to nurture a lot of close friendships. Now I do, and their numbers are increasing.

Linda

I regret that I have lost contact with many people whom I was close to in an earlier part of my life. Whatever happened to my once best friend, Marie; Joan, my great inspiration; and Barry with whom I was so in love? It seems that with each new phase – college, marriage, moving, divorce, moving again – I have lost some important connections. I enjoy meeting new people and some recent entries into my life have become friends, but I have come to especially value those few people who have known me for a long time. They are like emotional anchors in a world that often seems directionless and unpredictable. These days young people seem able to keep track of everyone they have ever known by using things like Facebook. I envy them.

⇒ Practical tips for polishing up your social skills:

Horchow, Sally and Roger Horchow. *The Art of Friendship: 70 Simple Rules for Making Meaningful Connections*. New York : St. Martin's Press, 2006.

Martinet, Jeanne. *The art of mingling: proven techniques for mastering any room*. New York: St. Martin's Griffin, 2006.

⇒ Discussion of issues for couples:

Vandervelde, Maryanne. *Retirement for Two: Everything you need to know to thrive together as long as you both shall live*. New York: Bantam Books, 2004.

⇒ For information to start a support group:

Sher, Barbara. and Annie Gottlieb. *Teamworks! : building support groups that guarantee success*. New York, NY: Warner Books, c1989.

Self Help Resource Centre: Starting a Self-Help Group.: http://www.selfhelp.on.ca/start.html

Happily Retired

chapter nine

Re-working

"All work and no play
makes Jack a dull boy,
All play and no work
makes Jack a mere toy."
Maria Edgeworth

Did you work in order to live or live in order to work? Retirement usually means that you no longer need to earn money to make living comfortable. The need to feel productive, however, does not go away. We thrive on applying skills and knowledge to accomplish something worthwhile.

Retirement offers real choice in terms of the kind of work undertaken and the degree to which you choose to stay involved in work-related projects. A Business Week Survey indicated that 67% of people reaching retirement age are still interested in doing some sort of work, but they are looking for positions which offer:

- More focus resulting in lower stress

- Flexibility and greater control over what, how, where and with whom the work is done

- Enjoyment derived from performing work, and

- The feeling of making a difference.

"Re-working" is about finding a new context for your skills. The psychological shock of going from a full-time career into full-time retirement can be less traumatic by continuing to work part time, by taking on occasional consulting contracts or by working as a volunteer.

The benefits of work are very similar before and after retirement, but your priorities with respect to work may now be very different.

Priority	Before Retirement	Now
Highest	$ to earn a living	Satisfying
	Time constraints	Fun
	Match for skills	Balance
	Balance/context	Related to other interests
	Satisfying	Time constraints
Lowest	Fun	$ to spend or save

Returning to Work

Opportunities for going back to paid work on your own terms are increasing as employers wrestle with how to handle the loss of experienced workers. The increased availability of work over the Internet is another opportunity for retirees, allowing us to work from a beach in Florida or a villa in Spain. For some, retirement can be an opportunity to explore a whole new line of work through self-employment.

"Golf was all I ever dreamed about. I knew all I'd do was golf once I quit the rat race. So when the pressure cooker got so overwhelming at my store manager job, I took the early retirement plan. And I golfed and golfed, but eventually needed more. So now I'm a high school baseball coach getting paid peanuts; just loving every single second of it."

Mike as quoted in
'What to Do With the Rest of Your Life' by Robin Ryan
www.robinryan.com

Pursuing some type of work in retirement theoretically should be less stressful than pursuing a career. You are no longer as driven by the need to earn and climb the corporate ladder. Some prefer to take on jobs that are exactly the opposite of the high profile, high pressure jobs they had prior to retiring. One successful corporate administrator discovered that a part-time job in a gardening store was relaxing, therapeutic and a great way to get to know people in his community. A former professional librarian decided to open a spa.

This allowed her to develop her latent business skills and to pursue a novel and creative venture that differed greatly from her original career path.

Consider your motivations for returning to work. Don't just "escape" back to the workplace before taking time to discover what is really important to you. A cashier's job at a retail store is fine if you like the hours and enjoy serving the public, but don't get trapped in a dead-end job that brings little in the way of satisfaction.

Do go back to work if . . .	Do NOT go back to work if . .
You want new opportunities to use your professional skills.	You have NOT YET carefully evaluated what matters to you.
You found your career stimulating and rewarding.	A job would significantly interfere with other appealing retirement opportunities
Work leaves you feeling energized and renewed.	A job would involve extra pressure on your time in the form of long drives, late hours, taking work home – remember, retirement should offer some level of personal freedom.
Work seems to offer new opportunities for expressing aspects of yourself that may have lain dormant in your previous working life (for example, starting a spa).	The work opportunities available to you do not dovetail with your personality and personal aspirations.
Work will provide a chance to spend time with amiable colleagues and co-workers filling a need for more social contact.	A job would interfere with opportunities to spend time with people who are important to you (a retired spouse, grandchildren, relatives or close friends.)
You are convinced that work offers an engaging way to spend your time.	Money is the only attraction – hold out for some kind of work that will also offer personal reward and still give you some control over your own time.

A little ingenuity and negotiating can allow you to have the best of both worlds. In some cases, you may find that you actually make more money than when you accepted the limitations of a standard working situation.

The Same but Different

After her husband had a narrow escape from a frightening medical condition, Myrna decided to retire from her professional responsibilities and really enjoy life. She and her husband invested in top of the line camping equipment and set out on a long cross-country road trip. That first year they spent a month in Asia, took a cruise to South America, and went on several shorter camping trips. Being fun-loving and resourceful, they had a good time and got all their household projects done as well. Myrna says, "I never get bored, but it was bothering me not to be doing something worthwhile. I caught myself pretending to be having a better time than I really was."

Within 18 months she was back at work. She carved out the part of her work that she most enjoyed and offered to job-share the custom-made job with another retiree. Her employer jumped at the opportunity to get her back.

Volunteering

"To share often and much . . . .
To know even one life
has breathed easier because you have lived,
this is to have succeeded."
Ralph Waldo Emerson
in Random Acts of Kindness

You may love to work, but not want a job and certainly not a boss. Volunteering your time informally or through any of a multitude of organizations can provide most of the benefits of work while maintaining control and flexibility. Volunteering is a chance to use your skills and may provide a new network of regular contacts.

The stereotype is that volunteering involves boring, unskilled work: stuffing envelopes for a charity fundraiser, driving little old ladies to doctors' appointments, organizing a rummage sale, or knocking on doors for a political candidate. These are all worthwhile and possibly enjoyable, but they are not your only options. Many really challenging opportunities are also available.

Because the work is voluntary, you have the freedom to choose what works best for you. With a bit of research and negotiating, you can find something that incorporates:

- Flexible hours

- Opportunity to gain new skills (e.g., setting up a Web site for a community group or organizing an event)

- Location close to home (or even work from home)

- Sharing work with a team

- Chance to travel

A recent study in Australia found that volunteers were among the most satisfied people in the country. They expressed happiness with their activities, work hours, a sense of connectedness to their community, and spirituality. The ability to tailor an unpaid placement to your personal interests and aptitudes is one of the reasons that volunteering offers a high level of satisfaction. Here are some examples:

- A professor with a life-long interest in film starts a local program to introduce aspiring film-makers to aspects of video-production. He successfully involves local professionals in this venture.

- H'Art is a program where volunteers involve adults with intellectual disabilities in painting, dancing, literacy and computer skills.

- A former teacher sees a need in the schools and initiates a program that will grow to 1400 volunteers helping school children learn new concepts in language and math.

- A retired veterinarian becomes active in a veterinary medical association. One of his most important initiatives is to establish a veterinary reserve that will mobilize the profession to provide expertise and services in response to animal health emergencies.

- An amateur cook who loves experimenting with new recipes takes on the task of preparing healthy frozen meals for a hates-to-cook friend with diabetes. The cook is building a collection of recipes that he hopes to eventually publish as a fundraiser for a local branch of the diabetes association.

- An amateur musician helps with organizing a local children's choir and serves as a flautist for the group.

- A retired business man offers support, advice and mentoring to business start-ups.

- A semi-retired woman devotes two hours each week to helping someone learn to read as part of a local literacy program.

- A former nurse and college administrator finds that she has become an invaluable resource for an agency running group homes for the elderly.

- A retired couple help run a local food bank through their church. Along with a number of other church members, they are part of a year-round rotation that keeps the food bank operational. Teams take turns handling donations and organizing distribution.

- An interior decorator uses her skills to transform a local women's shelter. She successfully involves family, friends and local businesses in the initiative.

- A man with a keen interest in history volunteers to be an exhibit interpreter for a museum exhibit on the Vikings.

- A professional historian offers his services to a local group restoring and researching the background of a heritage property in the community.

- A writer helps prepare public relations materials and a newsletter for a hospice in her community.

- A retired accountant helps low-income and people with disabilities prepare their income tax returns.

International Opportunities

Volunteering is gaining popularity among retirees who want their travel experiences to be something more than sight-seeing and sitting on a beach.

Executive Service Corps, British Executive Services (BESO) and Canadian Executive Services Organization (CESO) are examples of charitable organizations of experienced executives who offer their time as community advisors in areas such as financial management, business development and governance. Thousands of volunteers serve as mentors, advisors and trainers in areas including tourism, banking, information management and community planning. Volunteers give their time and expertise for a few weeks, while their travel costs and living expenses are covered.

A Personal Note

As a volunteer member of Canadian Executive Services Organization (CESO), I have mentored Inuit management trainees in Iqaluit, overhauled information management practices for a native office in Quebec, advised on the business plan for an on-line clearinghouse of tools for early childhood education for aboriginals, and reviewed a housing program. These projects helped me to freshen up and better appreciate my skills.

My most exotic posting was three months in Kingston, Jamaica where I taught internal financial auditors at a university how to do a management audit of their use of technology. I received no payment, but all expenses for my husband and me were covered. We got to know Jamaica and Jamaicans as no tourist ever could!

Julie

Cross Cultural Solutions has designed one of its programs specifically to attract volunteers who are over fifty. This agency places individuals in countries such as India, Ghana, Peru, China, Russia, Thailand, and Costa Rica. Although expenses are not covered, the placements provide a unique opportunity for immersion in a different culture and making a difference in the world.

The Virtuous Vacation

For two work-filled weeks we volunteered at a Costa Rican school — and in trying to teach the kids, we learned even more about ourselves.

Not only are we here by choice, but we've paid almost $2,500 each for the privilege. We're among the many Americans who are trading sightseeing for service, and immersing themselves in a country and its people.

"Most people who come here never see the real country," says Jose Ugalde, CCS's country director. "They arrive, they get on an air-conditioned bus, they go to an air-conditioned resort."

Ken Bud in The Virtuous Vacation
www.aarpmagazine.org

Going Local

Most communities offer an abundance of rewarding opportunities for volunteers. The request could be as simple as regularly assisting a friend or neighbor, organizing an annual community clean-up or serving on the board of a non-profit organization. Theatre companies, arts cooperatives, sports teams, musical groups and civic clubs may all potentially help you meet a personal goal or learn new skills.

The most important aspect of successfully volunteering is finding a good match between your interests and the kind of work that needs doing. You don't *need* to bring your unique skills to a particular project (although that may be ideal) – you may volunteer because you want a change and a new social context or want to feel that you are contributing to the community.

Volunteering can be rewarding and energizing, but it should fit well with your lifestyle and expectations. If you are looking for two hours each week with no strings attached, then helping at a local hospital or driving for Meals on Wheels could be ideal. If you are looking for more involvement in a community of like-minded people or for a situation where you can really make use of your skills, you may need to work at identifying an ideal placement.

On Giving Too Much

Volunteering may sound noble and selfless, but mainly it should be personally rewarding. Like employment, every relationship includes an implicit contract with expectations on all sides. Hard feelings arise when these expectations are not met. Satisfaction is far more likely if you are clear within yourself on what you expect in return and you communicate these expectations.

In some cases, volunteers are pushed to take on more work than they can comfortably handle – particularly if their skills are much in demand. At the other end of the spectrum are volunteers whose efforts are taken for granted. Both situations can lead to frustration and burnout.

Tips for Volunteering

- Consider the skills you have to offer.

- Focus on causes that are important to you.

- Look for a volunteer opportunity that can help you achieve a personal goal.

- If you volunteer with an agency, don't be put off by the request for an interview or security check. These indicate that the agency takes their volunteers seriously. Chances are an interview will also give you an opportunity to explore whether or not the volunteer placement is a good fit for you.

- If you don't want to commit your time to volunteering on a regular basis, consider helping out as a volunteer occasionally at a church fundraiser or community event.

When Life Volunteers You

Caring for elderly parents, or anyone else in need, can also be much like a full-time job. This responsibility can absorb significant amounts of time and energy. Being a caregiver can be tiring, stressful, emotionally draining, and often the effort is unrecognized. Care giving is a difficult role. Watching a loved one physically or mentally decline and assuming responsibility for their well-being can be unpleasant and scary. When that person is angry or resistant, the task is even harder. Financial issues and family disagreements may also arise. You may need to put your own life on hold.

If you are in such a situation, recognize and give yourself credit for the level of work involved. Knowing that you are needed and performing an important task can contribute to having a sense of engagement.

A Personal Note

We were fortunate to be retired with lots of discretionary time when my mother-in-law succumbed to inoperable cancer. During her final weeks, she was able to be at home with us. We had the opportunity to ease her final days and express our caring. That may sound noble, but it was actually a profound privilege to share intimacy, say what had gone unsaid, make peace with death, and forge closer ties with other family members. What would have been a terrible, and perhaps impossible, chore before retirement became a life-enriching experience.

Julie

Babysitting grandchildren is the other common opportunity for work that may or may not be discretionary. The job may range from sporadic episodes (while the parents take a trip, go to the movies or during emergencies) to a fulltime job, whether paid or not. Spending time with grandchildren can be rewarding, but consider how you can cut back on this task if you find it is interfering with other things you may want to do.

Locate a Web site for volunteering in your community. Use Google and search *volunteering + your city* or *"volunteer opportunities" + your city*. Locate at least three opportunities that you would find appealing – if not right now, at some point in your retirement. Use the postings to refine your thoughts about what kind of volunteer placement is a good fit for you.

Personal Reflections

Julie

My greatest joy has come from my many projects. I like to apply and build on my hard-won skills. As a result, my activities look a lot like work. One of my interests (applying big organization management practices to small businesses) slowly became a modest consulting business (coaching and preparing business plans for entrepreneurs).

Volunteer work has provided amazing opportunities for travel, deep connections, stretching my boundaries, and learning, all without the inconvenience of a boss. I like the feeling of serving the community. I became a trustee of the public library board, vice president of a local Freenet (an early public initiative to get people onto the Internet), organizer of a Home Business Association, volunteer Tai Chi instructor, coordinator of a lecture series for a seniors' group, and participated in many other worthy causes.

Big projects keep me interested and, I hope, interesting.

Linda

Some people have a slightly negative impression about volunteering. I know I do. I think the problem stems from the fact that on a number of occasions I have agreed to volunteer in contexts that did not really suit my skills or interests. It's easy to get roped into volunteer work out of a sense of duty or an inability to say no. Having said that, I really admire people who do volunteer. I once met a woman who as a volunteer gave haircuts to homeless men. She was very much appreciated by these men who otherwise had little opportunity for grooming, and she felt validated by performing this seemingly small service.

I think the trick is to find the right context for volunteering, something that holds personal meaning for you. I should try it again.

⇒ Ryan, Robin. ***What to Do With the Rest of Your Life: America's top career coach shows you how to find or create the job you'll love.*** Simon & Schuster, 2002

⇒ Stone, Marika and Howard. ***Too young to retire: 101 ways to start the rest of your life***. New York: Plume, 2004, c2002.

⇒ This site includes an extensive list of volunteer organizations and opportunities, including opportunities for volunteering abroad.

   Idealist.org: www.idealist.org/volunteer/vol_sites.html

⇒ **Employment Services for 50+:**
   http://retirementrevised.com/career/employment-resources-for-50-workers

⇒ An organization that is always looking for volunteers at all levels of skill

   Habitat for Humanity: http://www.habitat.org/

chapter ten

Get Learning

*"happiness also depends on . . . the feeling
that one is growing, improving. That process is,
by definition, a process of learning ...
One might conclude that learning is the pursuit
of happiness."*
Mihaly Csikszentmihaly

"Lifelong learning" was a phrase coined to describe the kind of studying needed to keep up with (or keep) your job at a time when computers seemed to be taking over. Did the enthusiasts mean retirees even then? What does learning offer us?

LOTS!

Learning is an essential component of engagement. It can be an avenue for making new friends, enhancing your life, and keeping your brain sharp!

Some people have a natural curiosity and instinctively love learning, but others have mixed feelings. All of us start out with a voracious appetite for learning, but formal education with its traditional "sit in your seat and don't make trouble" mentality may not have been an easy fit. A negative experience in school may be a lasting disincentive to wanting to learn in later life. Even the academically gifted may have been discouraged by the rat-race aspect of studying for grades.

If you have remained a keen learner throughout your life, you now have the luxury of exploring new avenues. But if you were turned off learning at some earlier point, be reassured that learning in retirement bears little relationship to classroom drills and it can be a chance to re-engage with the world.

In this chapter we talk about the opportunities for learning and the benefits of making learning a part of your life. Although a learning experience can be as simple as watching a documentary on television, our focus is more on the active pursuit of learning through continuing education classes, workshops, distance learning and self-directed learning.

"Do you realize how old I will be by the time I master the piano?"

"The same age you'll be if you don't!"

Polish Up Your Learning Skills

Although the emphasis on learning in retirement should be more on fun than on performance, making progress and deftly mastering new skills can help fuel a passion for learning. If in your earlier learning experience you were easily discouraged, educating yourself about recent research on how to learn more effectively might be beneficial.

Learning Styles

Understanding your learning style makes a big difference. Some of us are visual learners and retain information better if it is presented in pictures, diagrams and maps. Taking notes using colors or pictures to represent different concepts is helpful for visual learners. Those with a preference for auditory learning have strong listening skills.

Recording and playing back their notes helps them absorb information. Kinesthetic learners need to involve their whole bodies in learning; for example, pacing while reviewing notes for an exam. Social learners (who like to learn in a group), solitary learners, logical learners, and verbal learners all have their own style for most effectively absorbing and retaining information.

While these are preferences, most of us are a mix of different types and sometimes combining the use of more than one sensory type of input (audio and visual, for example) can really accelerate learning. This type of information about learning styles and study techniques can help you get the most out of a language class for travel, a financial planning seminar, computer instruction, or whatever you pursue.

Using the Internet

One of the most useful things you can do is to improve your Internet searching skills. In fact, a team of researchers recently reported that searching the Internet stimulates brain activity in the elderly and middle-aged and may help keep their minds sharp. Explore Google's advanced search "more" options or search engine tutorials.

A favorite spot for research is Wikipedia, an ongoing collaborative encyclopedia involving people from around the globe contributing information. Be sure to follow-up on some of the links to additional articles provided in many of the entries. You may even want to contribute.

Searching tip: To quickly find instructional Web content on a topic of your choice, search for the topic (in quotes if using more than one term) and the terms "FAQ" or "tutorial". Two examples would be *"digital photography" + FAQ* or *Spanish + tutorial*.

Learning Opportunities

Now you can set your own agenda with respect to what you learn, when and how. Learning is a way of exploring your interests and developing new skills that are useful and relevant to things you want to do. In addition, many novel opportunities and resources for learning are now available that don't involve sitting in a classroom.

Lecture Series

Lectures are informal learning opportunities, and often follow-up on a topic or issue is encouraged. Some colleges offer lecture series especially aimed at retirees. These focus on high-interest topics and fees are usually low. Many associations or agencies sponsor lectures on topics as diverse as art, music, health, history, politics and spirituality. Watch for announcements in your local newspaper.

The Great Courses (from the Teaching Company) is an example of a lecture series on DVD. The series includes courses in religion, philosophy, history, mathematics, science, fine arts, and economics. Lecturers are selected from the top 1% of professors based on such things as teaching awards and published evaluations. You could invite friends to join you in pursuing one of these courses. These can be purchased or found in a library.

Continuing Education Courses

Local school boards, municipalities and community groups offer a wide range of courses. While some of these still require you to show up on time and sit at a desk, the myriad of topics available are sufficiently attractive that the old-fashioned approach can easily be overlooked.

Examples:

- Line dancing
- Italian for travelers
- Renting a European villa with friends
- European history
- Thai cuisine
- Qigong (a set of breathing and movement exercises)
- Digital photography
- Genealogy

Check newspapers and libraries for courses and workshops in your area. Some universities also offer courses for seniors, at a reduced cost. These focus on high-interest topics and usually do not require writing papers, exams and the type of rigorous work necessary to earn a degree. But then again, you might want to work for a degree or formal certification in a whole new field. If you think you might want to pursue a more ambitious program of study, talk to a college counselor to find out what is involved and about options for studying part-time.

E-Learning

The Internet offers an amazing array of distance learning opportunities – some formal (courses offered by colleges and universities), and some not. Distance learning can be a chance to study topics that might not be readily available locally and to connect with people around the globe. E-learning offers a flexible study schedule. Even if distance is not an issue, some people just don't like driving to classes.

Basic computer skills and equipment are a prerequisite. Also, not all distance learning courses are well designed and as a learner you may feel isolated. Try an informal freebie or inexpensive offering before investing in a credit course.

Check out these sources for free e-learning content:

The Open University Open Learn:
http://www.open.ac.uk/openlearn

MIT Open Courseware:
http://ocw.mit.edu/OcwWeb/web/home/home/index.htm.
Teaching materials from 1800 university courses, some including videos and audio lectures. This is not an actual course since no instructor leads the process and you will not

be interacting with other students, but it can still be a rich learning resource.

iTunes University
You can download the iTunes software from www.itunes.com. Many free and other courses can be found in the iTunes Store through the iTunesU menu.

Personal tutor

A personal tutor or coach can be a wonderful asset when you are attempting to master something challenging. This is an ideal way to learn a musical instrument, learn new computer skills or master a complicated game like bridge.

Clubs and Discussion Groups

Getting together with friends or acquaintances is one of the most comfortable ways to learn something new. Investment clubs, wine tasting groups, and travel study groups are just a few examples. These provide entertainment and a pleasant social encounter as well as an opportunity to gain new knowledge. Book discussion groups are especially popular. The local library is a good place to find out about discussion groups in your community.

Virtual Communities

One of the most popular types of virtual community these days are blogs. Blogs (short for Web logs) are theme-driven areas on the Internet where one person or a group presents a topic and others have the opportunity to post comments and questions. Not all blogs have a learning focus, but some are devoted to topics such as photography, computers, cooking, the environment, knitting, music, writing, philosophy and personal development.

Explore some blog possibilities:

- Use Google's blog search (under "more")

- Blogs 101 by Rich Meislin provides a list of blogs to visit to get the feel of Web logs

  http://www.nytimes.com/ref/technology/blogs_101.html

- Check the New York Times' great selection

  http://www.nytimes.com/ref/topnews/blog-index.html

- Visit the Barnes and Noble Book Clubs at

  http://bookclubs.barnesandnoble.com

Learning Vacations

This is the perfect way to turn a vacation into something more than a quick sampling of tourist hot spots. Learning vacations serve a wide range of interests from water color painting or language immersion to golf camps, choir camps or furniture making. Cultural travel is a term used to describe group tours that include an education component, where you can learn about the history and culture of the place you are visiting.

Some examples:

- Elderhostel offers some great educational travel opportunities.

- Shawguides publishes *A Guide to Cultural Travel*.

- The Chautauqua Institution is a well-established (founded in 1874) adult education center and summer resort located in Chautauqua, New York.

There are several similar organizations in other locations. Each blends arts, education and recreation in a rich summer experience. You can stay for a day, a week, a month or more. Some offer 55+ weekend programs in the spring and fall.

Self-directed learning

You don't need to force-fit yourself into someone else's curriculum at considerable cost and inconvenience. With self-directed learning you decide what and how you want to learn. If you are already spending a certain amount of time "surfing" the Internet, you can turn this unfocussed time into an opportunity for learning something of value

Create a Personal Learning Plan. Creating a learning plan might seem grandiose if all you have in mind is the possibility of taking a wine-tasting class, but in this exercise start thinking about how you could actually make learning an important part of your retirement experience. Adding a learning component to almost anything that interests you can fuel your enthusiasm and spark new opportunities for engagement.

Choose a subject area.

Use your notebook or journal to respond to these questions:

- What interests you about the subject?

- What are possible ways of learning more about this?

- Which of these options is most attractive?

- What are some first steps you could take to get started?

- How will you know you've accomplished your learning goal?

- What are the things you need to do and when do you need to do them? Set up a schedule with benchmarks and deadlines if you feel it would increase your momentum.

Learning by doing

Tackling a project that requires you to learn new skills is an example of experiential learning. Setting up a solar energy system at your cottage is an example. If you have not done this before, you are bound to acquire new information and skills. Experiential learning may come from setting goals and identifying steps that you need to take to reach those goals; for example, becoming a better public speaker. Learning is part of exploring any new territory, with or without books. The next chapter explores learning opportunities through hobbies.

Don't let inhibitions or fear of failure stop you from learning something you might enjoy. You may think that if you did not learn to play a musical instrument, draw, dance, or even cook as a young person, it's too late to start. Not so. John Holt was an inspiring writer and educator. At the age of forty – with no previous musical training – he took up the cello, and it became a passion.

"If I could learn to play the cello well, as I thought I could, I could show by my own example that we all have greater powers than we think; that whatever we want to learn or learn to do, we probably can learn; that our lives and our possibilities are not determined and fixed by what happened to us when we were little, or by what experts say we can or cannot do."

John Holt in *Never Too Late*

Personal Reflections

Julie

Learning is one of my favorite activities. It is a valued by-product of nearly everything I do. Each bit of knowledge makes me feel more complete. I like the feeling in my head as the gears go through their paces. I love the feeling of adventure as one piece of information or insight leads to another. Learning is like dancing for the mind.

Linda

I have taken a number of e-learning courses. The possibilities are so amazing. I remember once stumbling into my office at 6 a.m. for an online text chat. I was still foggy-headed and sipping coffee to wake myself up, while participants half-way around the world were saying things like, "Well, this has been great, but time for me to get to bed." When you connect to other people all over the world in real time, it makes you realize that we really do live in a global world. The Internet makes learning opportunities almost boundless.

⇒ Leonard, George Burr. *Mastery: the keys to long-term success and fulfillment.*

⇒ Gross, Ronald. *Peak Learning: A Master Course in Learning How to Learn.* c. 1991, pub. Jeremy P. Tarcher, Inc.

⇒ Gross, Ronald. *The Independent Scholar's Handbook.* Berkeley, CA: Ten Speed Press, 1993

⇒ Learning Preferences:
www.learning-styles-online.com
www.ronaldgross.com/Tests.html

⇒ Study Techniques:
JCU Study Skills Online:
http://www.jcu.edu.au/office/tld/learningskills/mindmap/
How to Study.com: www.how-to-study.com/
Study Guides and Strategies: www.studygs.net

⇒ Learning Vacations:

Elderhostel: http: www.elderhostel.org/

ShawGuide's Guide to Cultural Travel:
http://culture.shawguides.com/

Chautauqua Institution in New York: www.ciweb.org/

Chautauqua in Lakeside Ohio: www.lakesideohio.com/.

⇒ Internet Search Tutorial:

Pandia Goalgetter's *A short and easy search engine tutorial*:
http://www.pandia.com/goalgetter/

chapter eleven

A New Take on Hobbies

*"When you're really engaged in a hobby you love,
you lose your sense of time and enter what's called
a flow state, and that restores your mind and
energy"*
Carol Kauffman, Harvard Medical School

Hobbies present an opportunity to combine the joys of learning with the accomplishments of work. They don't have to be useful or financially rewarding or even logical, but they do need to be pleasurable and interesting for you.

Some dismiss hobbies as a waste of time, something for people with nothing better to do or just for children. Remember that wood-burning kit? Don't deny yourself the immense possibilities for pleasure and engagement that can be found in a hobby just because somewhere along the line you developed a prejudice about the word. Instead, call it a passion, creative focus, avocation, or field of independent research.

Hobbies can:

- Enhance creativity
- Help build self-esteem
- Help develop self-confidence
- Improve concentration
- Build skills
- Foster learning
- Create opportunities for meeting new people.
- Provide fun
- Relieve stress

Hobbies usually start as casual interests and pleasurable pastimes. As you become more involved and take pride in your accomplishments, as well as enjoying the process, you move beyond dabbling to engagement.

Finding the right niche

Any activity or interest that you find pleasurable is a candidate for further involvement. The choices are limitless. The challenge in starting a hobby is how to narrow the choices to something that will sustain your interest and fit your lifestyle. (You may love dogs, but forget about dog breeding if you live in an apartment.)

Whatever you choose doesn't need to be a long term commitment. More likely, an initial choice will lead to new interests, ending in the most surprising opportunities to apply your skills, learn, build, deepen relationships, and be creative.

Most often, hobbies evolve naturally, but not always. Sometimes you need to kick start the process with a bit of research to find an area of activity that grabs and holds your attention. The antidote for inertia (or TV) is to choose an area and learn something about it.

What is available? Once you start looking, you will notice announcements about meetings, whole sections of the book store and library, friends talking about hobbies, and, of course, the many Internet sources.

Wikipedia lists hundreds of examples sorted into the following broad categories:

Amateur science-related	Interactive fiction
Animal-related	Internet-based hobbies
Arts and crafts	Literature
Collecting	Model (scale model) building
Computer-related	Music
Cooking	Observation
DIY (Do It Yourself)	Outdoor/nature activities
Electronics	Performing arts
Film-making	Photography
Games	Sports / physical activities
Gardening	Toys of some sophistication
Historical re-enactment	Transportation

You don't need to justify your choices of where to engage and you don't need to stick to your choices once made. Hobbies do need to be satisfying to you. Let's take a closer look at a few of the possibilities.

Collecting

We all have accumulated related objects: art, jewelry, clothing, souvenirs, photographs, books, recorded music. The result may be too much clutter. But collecting is different from just accumulating. It involves strategy, research, and presentation.

For Whom the Bells Toll

I met Bev at a party and asked what she did for fun. When she confessed to owning a collection of over a hundred bells, I was ready to pretend that I needed to be somewhere else. What could be more boring? Fortunately, I was slow to make an exit.

Bev, like me, enjoys travel. While I tend to stick to run-of-the-mill sights that everyone else visits, Bev goes looking for bells in out of the way shops. She ends up discovering quaint neighborhoods, talking to shopkeepers, chatting with other shoppers, and having all kinds of adventures on the excuse of looking for bells to buy. She gets in touch with other collectors so that she can see their collections when she is in town, and ends up going out for tapas with a group of the collector's friends. What a neat way to add an extra twist to a travel adventure.

Julie

Clues for what to collect can be found in items already in your possession. Common categories for collections are coins, stamps, art, music, butterflies, sports cards, figurines, antiques, toys, and even stories. But collecting isn't really about the items that are collected, it is more often a framework for exploring history, art, music, literature or science. Stamp collectors are most often interested in the story behind those stamps; they are interested in the events, people and places that are represented in these miniature works of art.

A Lifelong Stamp Collector

"Stamp Collecting dispels boredom, enlarges our vision, broadens our knowledge, makes us better citizens and in innumerable ways, enriches our lives."

Franklin Delano Roosevelt

Collecting can lead to some interesting adventures as you seek opportunities to add to your collection. The most popular areas for collecting are well organized with publications, Web sites and stores dedicated to the pursuit. Clubs and shows add a social dimension as well as provide information and new ideas.

Start by asking questions. If you have always had an interest in antiques, but have no idea of how this might translate into a collection, visit antique stores and notice what catches your eye – jewelry, lampshades, doorknobs, old tools. Often antique store owners are experts so take the time to pick their brains.

Use your collection as an excuse to branch out. Some successful collectors have even turned their collections into a part-time business. Collecting isn't for everyone but it can be a satisfying route to engagement if there is a focus that appeals to you.

Caution!

Collecting can become compulsive and expensive. Be selective and set a budget. Set your own rules, buy what appeals to you, but avoid the temptation to go beyond your budget just because it's part of a series or very rare. Inform heirs of the value of the collection and how to realize that value.

Hobbies and Creativity

Creativity is a particularly rewarding driver for many pursuits. Writing, weaving, gourmet cooking, photography, art, model building, performing, and many other activities provide opportunities for creative expression. They are a source of personal satisfaction and allow you to give a piece of yourself to the world.

To be truly engaging a hobby must involve more than just dabbling. This is particularly true for hobbies involving creativity, since creative expression requires effort and concentration. While hobbies are meant to be fun, there is real work involved in building skills in areas such as painting, photography, writing or ballroom dancing. The reward for such effort is engagement and the enjoyment that comes with self-expression.

Miniature Worlds

Models are accurate representations of real-world objects, but at a reduced scale: cars, airplanes, doll houses, office towers, a medieval tournament or miniature soldiers in a battle. Making miniatures is a way of studying something in depth.

Far from being toys, models are used in many professional disciplines. Scientists use them as a research tool. Architectural models show relationships within the structure and to the environment. Simulations are used to study everything from epidemiology to weather patterns to the design of ergonomic chairs. Part of the satisfaction derived from creating a model stems from capturing true-to-life detail.

Model railroaders have a fascination with trains. Their collections typically include scale models of locomotives, railroad cars, tracks signals, bridges, scenery and miniature villages. Acquiring components and building elaborate layouts provides many hours of engagement and enjoyment for these collectors. Many strive for historically accurate representations.

A class is a good way to get started on a creative hobby. This can be useful even if you are already familiar with basic techniques. Taking a class is one way to make a commitment. For example, if you learned to play the piano at an earlier point in your life and want to pursue this again, taking a few lessons can get you back in the game if there is a risk that studying piano on your own would be hit and miss.

Once started, decide how you want to pursue your hobby. Creative hobbies can be private sources of enjoyment – or they can involve competing, selling your creative works, or joining a group. Groups are a good way to learn from others and become more involved.

Becoming an Expert

Engagement is enjoyment of the process as much as the results. Hobbies that involve becoming knowledgeable about some field of interest are primarily about the process. Becoming an expert at anything requires focusing and building knowledge step-by-step. Astronomy, computers, historical re-enactment, genealogy, scrabble and bridge are examples of hobbies where the fun is in the doing. Eventually interest morphs into expertise. Frequently, you will discover side benefits as well: new skills, travel, social opportunities and the satisfaction of gaining new knowledge.

Checking Out the Family Tree

Become an expert on your own heritage. Genealogy involves research into historical records, judgment to assess the quality of sources, analysis to assemble indirect or circumstantial evidence, and imagination to flesh out and integrate the stories that emerge. The more you become immersed in the details, the more tempting it is to weave the details into a story that can be shared among family members.

The process provides a focus. You meet distant relatives with an instant sense of connection and something to talk about. Traveling becomes more engaging because you are looking for specifics that take you off the beaten track and connect you to the locals.

Heading Outdoors

Some hobbies offer the added bonus of fresh air and exercise. Gardening and golf are two of the most popular hobbies. They offer wonderful possibilities for those key ingredients for engagement such as building on strengths, learning and feeling challenged (like battling garden slugs). Even if you are not keen on gardening or golf, choose from many other outdoor hobbies, from kayaking, backpacking or fishing to geo-caching, birding or walking to improve fitness and explore new terrain.

"I remember in grammar school the teacher asked if anyone had any hobbies. I was the only one with any hobbies, and I had every hobby there was. There was no hobby I didn't have, name anything, no matter how esoteric, I had found it and dabbled in it. I could have given everyone a hobby and still had 40 or 50 to take home."

Cormac McCarthy, Pulitzer Prize Winning Author

Choose a hobby, maybe one you don't know much about, but that you think you might enjoy and research it. Ideally, find a person or a group involved in this activity and find out how they got involved and what advice they have for someone just getting started. Visiting a specialty store (such as an antique shop) or going to an event (such as a presentation or trade show) might be enough to get you hooked.

Personal Reflections

Julie

My forms of engagement seem to fit best within the categories of relationships, re-working, and learning. I take on long-term projects (like this book), but hobbies seem to provide a sort of unifying theme that I am missing. Getting a bona fide hobby, maybe painting, is on my to-do list.

Linda

I was one of those with a bias against hobbies. After exploring the topic and discovering what it is about hobbies that some people find so rewarding, I am a convert. I am intrigued by the keen fascination and boundless enthusiasm many people have for their hobbies.

I too would like to frame some part of the world and turn it into a personal domain. This was brought home to me once when I attended a Civil War historical re-enactment. Through creativity and social interaction, this historical event was made so real for the people involved, and their passion was infectious.

I know hobbies exist for the very reason that they are engaging, and that they don't require us to accomplish something grand as part of our involvement. Since I have this hang-up about needing to accomplish things, I think I should get a hobby.

chapter twelve

Finding Meaning

"Time often resembles a fine gold powder that we distractedly allow to slip through our fingers without ever realizing it. Put to good use, it is the shuttle we pass through the weft of our days to weave the fabric of a meaningful life."
*Matthieu Ricard, **Happiness***

A central motivating force in life is the search for meaning. Sensual pleasures are fleeting, one-dimensional. Engagement adds another dimension generating more lasting satisfaction. Engagement requires you to move beyond simple pleasure to a level of involvement that required learning or fostered self-growth. Finding meaning forces you to stretch beyond engagement. Meaning provides depth and gives staying power to happiness in a highly personal way.

In retirement, some important sources of meaning shift. Career achievement is no longer a central motivator. If your children are grown, your relationship to them may remain a source of meaning, but your day-to-day involvement in their lives is much less than when they were younger. If church-going or community involvement has become a habit, rather than providing a vital and continuing sense of meaning, you will probably sense the need for renewal.

Meaning permeates life in the form of values, love, nature, beauty, cultural identity, and philosophy. Your path to meaning will be specific to you. It will involve some combination of inner growth and connecting outward. Just as engagement flows from getting more involved with what gives you pleasure, meaning often evolves naturally from areas of engagement.

Reaching Out

Finding meaning commonly involves connecting outward beyond ourselves. Connecting to others in a heartfelt way, giving a piece of yourself in the form of an altruistic act; sharing wisdom, and caring all contribute meaning.

Love

Love and meaning are closely intertwined. Being loved makes us feel like we matter. Giving love is even more powerful. The greater the scope and depth of who and what you love, the more likely that you will experience your life as meaningful and happy. The difficulty we sometimes face is in understanding the how, what and why of love. Most of us recognize love when we experience it, but explaining how those feelings come about and making them happen is tricky. We love those who are close to us and with whom we share an emotional bond.

Love seems to occur most easily when we discover aspects of ourselves through a relationship. Grandchildren are often cited as a source of love and fulfillment among retirees, although we can't always explain why. One devoted grandmother says, "Seeing bits of myself and my daughter in the grandchildren moves me at a level I just can't explain. Not just physical attributes, but little mannerisms have that effect." Genetic continuity is not the primary factor here. Interactions with adopted children or grandchildren can inspire similar feelings of connection – they validate us; they are a part of

our lives. Neither is having close regular contact a requirement for love to flourish. Pure, unconditional love can be present even when loved ones are separated by distance or death. The underlying meaning, aside from the opportunity to love and be loved, seems to come from a sense of continuity and renewal of life.

Many aspects of our lives are centered upon our most intimate relationships. They are a source of joy, but relying exclusively on your love of a few individuals for a sense of meaning creates a vulnerability. With age, intimates (a partner and close friends) are more likely to become ill or die. Aside from the huge challenge of dealing with grief, these losses can undermine our sense of purpose. Similarly, our sense of purpose is diminished as our grown children disengage from our lives and need us less and less. All love relationships change over time, but love as a source of meaning in our lives is not lost if we recognize that love can extend beyond family, pets and close friends. A love of nature, beauty, ideas, history, the earth, and mankind also connects and nourishes.

Love also manifests when we make ourselves available in an abiding way to someone who needs us. Caring for an elderly relative or loved one with a disability helps us feel love and experience meaning. Selflessly caring for someone else affirms our humanity and fosters a feeling of connection to something greater than ourselves. Through giving, receiving, and opening our hearts we experience love and create meaning in our lives.

Service

Although love is most often experienced as a deep personal bond that engenders feelings of generosity, closeness and warmth; love can also be expressed through community service, causes and mentoring. When our caring extends beyond family and close friends, we forge a deeper connection with all of humanity.

The desire to serve comes from caring enough to want to make a difference. The difference can range from a small "random act of kindness" to saving a life or changing the world. Contributing is inherent to many love relationships – we make a big difference to the people and things we love and we frequently express our love by giving of ourselves. Your career probably required helping individuals, the community, or at least your employer. Retirement also offers many opportunities to serve.

Now the amount, type and target area of service is your choice. Choosing not to serve is an equally valid choice. It is, however, one excellent antidote for feeling irrelevant.

Communities

Communities are groups with a common bond. We derive meaning when we are attentive to the needs of communities that matter to us and generous in our response. Your communities may include an extended family, your neighborhood, church, political parties, volunteer organizations, and formal or informal clubs or social groups. In a more abstract way, the country and even the broader world are communities. Although these are not intimate bonds, communities provide connection and each has needs. Working to serve some of those needs can provide pleasure and engagement. If you also see value in the community and see that your efforts add to that value, then you will experience meaning.

In rare instances, you may offer transformative, heroic contributions to your communities, but your efforts are more likely to be in the form of offering to drive a neighbor to a medical appointment or donating to a local food bank. All of these make a difference and feel good. Don't overlook the value of small, simple acts of giving which are the lifeblood of most communities.

> "If our lives are dedicated . . . to enhancing the welfare of everyone we contact, our lives can never lose meaning. If the purpose of our life, on the other hand, is financial success, what happens after it is attained?"
>
> David R. Hawkins in *Power vs. Force*

Causes

> "*Never doubt that a small group of thoughtful, committed citizens can change the world. Indeed, it is the only thing that ever has.*"
> *Margaret Mead*

Reaching out can also take the form of tackling pervasive social problems. The headlines of any newspaper remind us daily of environmental issues, poverty, drug abuse, and violence. Working adults are, for the most part, preoccupied with the urgencies of their lives. Politicians and executives are under pressure to provide largely cosmetic quick fixes. Retirees are in a unique position to make a real difference. We have the perspective, skills, and especially freedom to think long-term.

The sheer numbers of fresh retirees over the next ten or fifteen years means that collectively we can have a huge impact if enough of us make an effort to change the world for the better. Retirement provides the opportunity to resurrect the passionate values expressed in the sixties – caring about our communities, caring about the broader world, sharing what we had with others, and promoting peace and love. Now may be a good time to renew the values of "peace and love".

Think of the lasting impact made by activists in the fields of public health (anti-smoking, breast cancer screening), quality of life (livable cities, resisting big box stores, slow food movement, bicycle paths), public safety (MADD), philosophy (human rights), the environment (recycling, reducing pesticides), and many more. All of these initiatives came about through the efforts of individuals driven by a sense of purpose.

The Journey of Peace Pilgrim

From 1953 to 1981 a silver haired woman calling herself only "Peace Pilgrim" walked more than 25,000 miles on a personal pilgrimage for peace. She vowed to "remain a wanderer until mankind has learned the way of peace, walking until given shelter and fasting until given food." In the course of her 28 year pilgrimage she touched the hearts, minds, and lives of thousands of individuals all across North America. Her message was both simple and profound. It continues to inspire people all over the world:

> "This is the way of peace:
> Overcome evil with good,
> and falsehood with truth,
> and hatred with love."
> ....Peace Pilgrim

From the Peace Pilgrim and Friends of Peace Pilgrim Website: http://www.peacepilgrim.com/

Inertia rather than indifference may cause us to turn our attention elsewhere when we are made aware of problems in our society. The drive to improve something you see happening and a belief that you can have an impact leads to opportunities to leave a legacy. Contributions can be large or small with success measured on your own terms.

Identify a cause that interests you – not necessarily a current involvement, just something in the world that you would change if you could. Write down your thoughts about this issue and its impact on the world. Consider how this situation affects your own life. Write down one thing you could do in the next month that could help improve the situation (write a letter, make a donation, join a group, etc.). Add that action to your to-do list.

Modeling & Mentoring

Traditionally, the elders of a society were valued for their wisdom gathered from experience and observation. They were the keepers of traditions with the responsibility for cultural guidance, teachings, ceremonies, activities and events. They were the healers and arbitrators of disputes. Age alone did not qualify an individual as an elder. He or she could be someone younger who earned the respect of their community by enriching its spiritual development.

Age in itself certainly does not earn much respect in our society, but all of us have learned so much in our journey from twenty-something to sixty-something. At a minimum, we can set a good example of how to live well. We can "hold the centre" with a clear sense of values and by speaking the truth about our world.

The greatest compliment to a would-be elder is when someone notices that you have something to offer and asks to be mentored.

A Personal Note

One of the joys of my life is the opportunity to help others benefit from my hard-earned lessons. Working as a coach helps me feel validated and honored.

At a particularly challenging time in his work, my son's friend, Tom, asked if I would be willing to formally become his coach. Tom and I had gotten to know one another, and he thought I might have some wisdom to impart. He not only wanted guidance with work-related problems, but wanted to learn some of the skills and balance and attitudes he had observed in me. We agreed on how to do this: a written agreement; periodic reviews; regular contact by phone, email, instant messaging and sometimes in person; permission to be blunt; obligation to be forthcoming. After nearly three years, Tom is proud and pleased with his development: "...working with you has been a HUGE help for me!! ...it has helped me find direction!"

Julie

Reaching Inward

Meaning comes from a sense of connectedness and contribution. But the connections we make are not always directed towards the world outside of ourselves. The most challenging connections are available when you reach within and connect to the realm of spirit. We connect to spirit through creativity, through mastery and through intentional spiritual practice.

The Spiritual Retiree

"I "retired" when I was 38. It was brought about by a spiritual crisis. I could not imagine continuing to live in the same way. I realized that I had attempted to "fit in" by having a career, a 9 – 5 job, fixed vacation days, by studying what I was supposed to learn and doing tasks that were assigned by someone else.

Surely my soul had desires, the pursuit of which would lead to a deeper sense of fulfillment! I constructed some guidelines for myself as I jumped into the unknown:

1) I would ask myself what I wanted (it could be as simple as "do I really want to go for a walk, or am I going because I think I need the exercise?"). I would pay attention to how I felt.

2) I would never again study something just because someone else told me I should.

3) I would give myself a break from asking "where will this lead?" I would just go where my desires took me.

4) I would commit myself whole-heartedly to an unknown path. This meant that I would have to trust myself and trust that there were unseen forces that would assist me.

5) I would live within my means so that financial pressures wouldn't force me into doing what I didn't want to do.

I began to meditate daily. This practice lead to my questioning a lot of assumptions I'd made about myself; it lead me to realizing that I hadn't really taken responsibility for my experience of life. I found that going deeply inward resulted in a completely different outward reality – that the outer was only a *reflection* of the inner.

Now, it seems amazing to me that I have the life I have. *My* desire was to integrate work, play, friendship, service and spirituality. There are elements of each in most things I do. I see life as a collaboration between my conscious self and spirit."

Ruth Redekop
Accountant, Bodyworker, & Meditation Teacher
www.ruthredekop.com

Reaching inward for meaning is a huge subject and highly individual. Here we will just touch on some of the forms that quest might take.

Creativity

Personal expression seems to foster a sense of wholeness. Why and how is not obvious, but the effect is profound.

On Creativity

"Painting and singing are the natural expression of who I am. I have a strong spiritual awareness of God as Creator dwelling within me. Expressing creatively connects me to that authentic, divine aspect of myself. I need to express in witnessable form what I am feeling, thinking, and being in the moment.

I've had this urge for as long as I can remember, but it was a stumbling and sometimes painful process until I matured into self-love. Now I use my creativity as a bridge to connect with myself, God, and other people. It gives my life meaning."

Patricia Collier, Artist in Gibsons Landing, BC

While many activities can be considered creative endeavors, the litmus test for creativity as a means for forming a spiritual connection is having a sense of tapping into a broader world of wonderment and beauty. Creativity is not limited to producing fine art. Avid gardeners feel a closeness to nature and are motivated by a desire to create something beautiful. Singing in a choir similarly involves creative expression, and again, there is a striving toward beauty and towards something larger than ourselves. Finding sources of creativity and allowing ourselves to be touched by the beauty of life can be metaphors for prayer. Many things done with reverence and love can be sources of creativity. Our ultimate creation is our own lives using the raw materials of experiences, relationships, skills and values.

Mastery

Mastery is the antithesis of a quick-fix mentality. It is that subtle extra that causes us to feels a deep connection. Compare an Olympic athlete to one who is merely competent; someone who does Tai Chi a few times a week to one who has incorporated it into body and life; a Glen Gould to a good piano player.

Mastery requires a combination of effort and giftedness. While excelling at an exceptional level may be rare, we can still learn something from the effort and involvement apparent in those who become masters. On an individual level, we achieve mastery when we reach beyond our boundaries and work toward accomplishing something that we never thought we could.

Meaning can come from striving and moving forward – sometimes towards personal mastery, but other times towards the accomplishment of a challenging task that holds meaning because it is aligned with an important value or something we care about deeply.

"Goals ... are important, but they exist in the future and the past. ,. . . Practice, the path of mastery, exists only in the present. You can see it, hear it, smell it, feel it. To love the plateau is to love the eternal now, to enjoy the inevitable spurts of progress and the fruits of accomplishment, then ... to accept the new plateau that waits just beyond them. To love the plateau is to love what is most essential and enduring in your life."

George Leonard
Author and Aikido Master

Spiritual Practice

The quest for spiritual growth is the ultimate form of connection.

This is the realm of philosophers, theologians and gurus, and most of them struggle for years to get it right. Our secular society largely ignores the need for a connection to a higher presence. Yet most of us still feel a need to experience a connection to something that transcends the banalities of everyday power struggles, conflict and commercialism. We long for access to a realm of consciousness where we might find wholeness and truth. Spiritual work requires focused intent and concentration.

At this stage of your life, you may choose to delve more deeply into the rituals and traditions of an organized religion. You may choose to experiment with one of the many forms of meditation. Meditation can be done individually or as part of a group practice. Twelve-step programs such as Alcoholics Anonymous are paths to spiritual healing. Your path may lead you to get into closer touch with nature or to begin a personal quest.

Lessons from the Camino

For many, walking El Camino de Santiago has been life-transforming. Over the past millennium, thousands from all over the world have made the pilgrimage to a shrine in Spain called Santiago de Compostela.

"When we become totally responsible for our decisions, personal awareness increases. The Camino experience forced me to see myself under a microscope, and I quickly discovered what works and what doesn't for me. The lessons I learned on the path will always be with me. I'll remember how I overcame physical challenges, dealt with my fear, and made new friends. As a result, I've identified a new, more compatible path that will take me to what I need for myself and have a better life. . . . We can all benefit from a learning experience like that of the Camino . . . . It teaches us to stop listening to negative internal voices and start leading from the heart. When we are self-aware and self-confident, we smile more often and laugh a little longer. And we believe that we are capable of anything."

Brooke Broadbent
Pilgrim, Coach, Author

Spiritual seeking is a part of the human experience. It involves recognizing and experiencing love in the universe. Choose according to what draws you. Like everything else, spiritual seeking begins with a willingness to take the first step. If you dig deeply enough, you will find meaning.

"Ultimately, man should not ask what the meaning of his life is, but rather he must recognize that it is he who is asked. In a word, each man is questioned by life; and he can only answer to life by answering for his own life; to life he can only answer by being responsible."

Viktor Frankl
Holocaust Survivor, Author, Psychotherapist

Personal Reflections

Julie

My sense of having meaning seems to come and go like the tides. I have observed in others the value of each of the categories of seeking meaning discussed in this chapter. I have dabbled in them all and experienced some subtle contentment with how I fit into the universe, at least on good days. Is that enough to claim that I've found meaning?

Meditation is an example of my dabbling. I have found great value in the Light Work, A Course in Miracles and even my own no-name form of meditation. Although I have experienced the benefits of a regular discipline, I go through periods when it feels like too much trouble and I do not consistently stick with it. The search continues.

Linda

I think that seeking meaning takes a certain amount of personal courage. It means resisting distractions, and opening yourself to a world beyond narrow self-interest. It means transcending complacency and stretching beyond your comfort zone. I'm not sure I am ready for all that, but I'm working on it.

⇒ Zukav, Gary. *The seat of the soul.* New York: Free Press, 2007, c1989

⇒ Leonard, George Burr. *Mastery: The keys to success and long-term fulfillment.* New York, N.Y.: Dutton, c1991.

⇒ Ricard, Matthieu, trans. Jesse Browner. *Happiness: a guide to developing life's most important skill.* New York: Little, Brown and Company, 2006.

⇒ Gawain, Shakti with Laurel King. *Living in the light: a guide to personal and planetary transformation.* Novato, CA : New World Library, c1998.

⇒ *A Course in Miracles: Workbook for Students.* New York, N.Y.: Viking: Foundation for Inner Peace, 1996.

⇒ Gibran, Kahlil. *The Prophet.* London : Heinemann, c1993.

⇒ Walsch , Neale Donald. *Conversations with God : an uncommon dialogue.* New York : G.P. Putnam's Sons, 1996-

⇒ Hawkins, David R. *Power vs. force : the hidden determinants of human behavior* . Carlsbad, Calif. : Hay House, 2002.

⇒ The Global Dialogue Institute: http://global-dialogue.com/

⇒ This movie provided an excellent illustration of how giving love might be more rewarding than receiving it

> *Marvin's Room.* [Burbank, Calif.] : Miramax Home Entertainment, c1997. Director: Jerry Zaks; screenplay by Scott McPherson.

chapter thirteen

Free to Be – You and Me

"Be Yourself. Everyone Else Is Taken!"
Charles Shultz

You are now free to pursue a life that is uniquely meaningful and rewarding for you. Retirement is a genuine opportunity to:

- Start fresh

- Discover who you are

- Do what you most enjoy

- Build on your accomplishments

- Make new friends

- Earn and learn – or not

- Make your own rules

- Fulfill lifelong dreams

- Make a difference

Meanwhile, freedom is scary. Self-exploration is sometimes frightening or at least uncomfortable. Venturing into the unknown is also intimidating. Ironically, we feel most alive when we stretch ourselves, take risks and explore unfamiliar territory.

You will likely discover this has been true for much of your life. Our senses are heightened, and we are challenged and energized by new ventures: starting school, starting a new job, moving into a new home, having a baby, taking a trip. Frequently, excitement or a strong sense of "needing to get on with it" overrides "scary". The same should be true of retirement, and it is – once we have managed to push past fear and recognize the tremendous opportunity beyond the door that has just opened.

The central challenge in retirement is to make satisfying choices about how to spend your time. Perhaps you started with the conviction that keeping busy is the secret to a happy retirement, and now you have discovered that busyness on its own is not enough to satisfy the soul. The "doldrums" are a sure signal that change is needed. Consciously pursuing and balancing pleasurable activities with those that offer engagement and, ideally, some that are a source of meaning is the secret to a rich, enduring and happy retirement life.

Getting the right mix is as significant as specific choices about how you will spend your time. Restlessness, dissatisfaction and boredom are signs that some element in the pleasure, engagement and meaning formula needs attention.

In a sense, you are starting fresh, but on a solid foundation of experience. If you allow yourself to let go of others' expectations and find your authentic self, the future can be about living a life where dreams come to you and opportunities abound.

The Big Picture

Pursuing happiness in your own life can also have a positive impact on the world around you. The tidal wave of boomers has already started to change the nature of retirement and the possibilities are exciting. Our generation has the potential to inspire social change if we choose to turn our attention to people, to causes and to the creation of beauty. Has the world ever had such a large leisure class with health, energy and experience?

Through our initiative, society as a whole may gain in the form of:

- A cultural renaissance as artists and thinkers are freed from their previous obscurity in the workforce

- Volunteers who are in a position to tackle problems at the level of root causes

- Leaders free to act from conscience

- Good role models and mentors for the next generation

- Contributions that emerge from integrity and authenticity

We have the opportunity to engage with the world in ways that are deeply meaningful and transformative.

What's Next?

Though the specifics may vary, the truly important aspects of our lives are about family, relationships, community involvement, good health, our relationship to nature and spending time on interesting and meaningful activities. In retirement, we are fortunate to have stepped off the treadmill that often keeps us from fully engaging in these facets of our lives. We can allow ourselves to become more deeply involved in our authentic selves.

If you are keeping a journal and have taken time to do some of the exercises included in the previous chapters, you probably already have some ideas about aspects of your life that need adjustment. You understand the importance of introspection, experimentation and optimism. Hopefully, you have a good sense of how much you may need to beef up opportunities for pleasure, go to the next level with engagement and pursue greater meaning. These three elements can be used to assess and fine-tune many different aspects of your life. The happiness formula and strategies provide a framework and tools that you can use to build a happy retirement.

You are now free of many of the former restraints on your individuality and are relieved of many urgent, externally imposed priorities. That is not to say that urgent and important situations such as a health crisis or a loved one in need won't constrain your options, but even then you have choices.

You can set priorities and focus on what matters to you. You can seek out day-to-day experiences that bring a variety of pleasures and engagements. You can savor those things that bring meaning into your life. Ultimately happiness is a highly personal choice you make moment by moment.

What's next? You choose!

Personal Reflections

Julie

I was suffering from a mild case of the doldrums when Linda approached me with the idea of collaborating on this book. It has provided many months of intense engagement and a taste of meaning as well. This has been an opportunity to gather the bits and pieces of myself. I now have a much better appreciation of how truly unique we each are in our perceptions and priorities, thanks largely to Linda's willingness to explore and challenge me. Each life is truly a work of art and that becomes most evident among retirees who exercise their freedom to be themselves.

I have been exploring ideas to find a balance of pleasure, engagement and meaning for myself. I am often happy.

I wish you daily smiles and laughter, quiet pride and gratitude, and knowledge that you matter.

Linda

A confession: From day one, Julie and I seemed to disagree about so many things. Who would have thought the topic retirement could be so controversial? While it was tempting on occasion to just give up, we persisted. That meant compromise. We had to think deeply about the issues people face in retirement and in many cases, our disagreements lead to some interesting opportunities for new perspectives and personal growth.

Both of us have been changed by this experience. We think that our struggles may have allowed us to approach some truths about retirement – what works, what doesn't and why. I have begun to reshape my life around the principles of the happiness formula and it is both exciting – and a relief. I have been able to get rid of my notion that my self-worth is tied to accomplishments and the need to be useful all the time. There are so many different facets of life to explore. Writing the book has helped me discover some wonderful new possiblities. I so hope that what we have written has inspired the same for you.

To be continued

We hope that this book will be the beginning of a dialogue. Please visit our Web site at

http://www.happily-retired.com

to continue the discussion.

Acknowledgements

We would like to thank the many friends and acquaintances who discussed, challenged, and informed our ideas about retirement. We are particularly grateful to those who demonstrate how to live well. We look forward to continuing the conversations with you, the reader.

Special thanks to individuals who gently reviewed and greatly enhanced our drafts of the manuscript: Ruth Redekop, Carole Baker, Jack Stilborn, Denise Dittberner, Patricia Santos, Judy Cedar, Donna Neff and Beverley Scott (who planted the seed that was the inspiration for this project).

We soon learned that creating and making a success of a book requires a range of skills that stretch well beyond writing. Many thanks to those who helped to fill some of our gaps: Patricia Santos (marketing), Donna Neff (editing), and Ruth Redekop (providing a broad perspective on spiritual searching from her years of teaching).

Artwork

The original line drawings contributed by British Columbia artist, Patricia Collier, made a wonderful addition to our text. She magically captured the mood we wanted to convey.

Additional drawings were provided by graphic designer, Kristin Kashyap, who created the exercise and resource icons, the busy bee in chapter 2, and the Enneagram diagram in chapter 3.

The portrait photograph of Julie is by S.R. Gour Photography.

Rights to use other photographs and drawings were purchased from Dreamstime.com:

Cover – Bubbles © Igor Dmitriev

Chapter 2 Work Upsides

- Applause © Pressmaster

- Valuable © Teresa Levite

Chapter 2 Work Downsides

- Chains © Soldeandalucia

- Weight of the world © Sarah Nicholl

Chapter 2 Retirement Downsides

- Big clock © Clicktrick

- Cracked Ground in Death Valley © Ron Chapple Studios

- No old folks ©Designalldone

Chapter 2 RetirementUpsides

- Grandfather reading © Mcininch

- Tropics ©Michael Guirguis

CPSIA information can be obtained at www.ICGtesting.com
Printed in the USA
LVOW101832291111

257009LV00004B/66/P